These Things:
A Reference Manual for Discipleship –
An Elementary Understanding of the
Faith Once Delivered

These Things:
A Reference Manual for Discipleship – An Elementary Understanding of the Faith Once Delivered

Rev. William Kyle Volkmer

Second Edition
The Passionate Few
2017

First Printing: May 2016
Second Edition: October 2017

ISBN 978-1-365-20586-6

The Passionate Few
10907 W Loop 1604 N
San Antonio, TX 78254

www.thepassionatefew.com

To Beth
Wife, encourager, helper, and beloved best friend

But Jesus said to him, "No one, having put his hand to the plow, and looking back, is fit for the kingdom of God." Luke 9:62

Contents

Foreword

A.W. Tozer said, "Were we able to extract from any man a complete answer to the question, 'What comes into your mind when you think about God?' we might predict with certainty the future of that man." In other words, what we think about who God is and what he is like determines our destiny. A healthy community of faith is built on the solid foundation of truth and Biblical literacy. William Volkmer has spent the last decade faithfully gathering, practicing, and implementing the tools of discipleship in both university and church settings. *These Things* is a timely compilation of these essentials of Christianity and a healthy springboard into a rich devotional life for believers of any age.

— Reverend Eli Gautreaux
      Director of University Student Ministries for the South Texas
      District Assemblies of God

An erosion of values and a compromising spirit in the world is influencing the church. God has anointed Kyle to prophetically teach rightly the whole council of the Bible and train God's people for ministry. This book is the overflow of his heart and life spent in God's service. "Wisdom is proven right by her children." Over the last decade, I've personally witnessed the manifest power of God in Kyle's life and ministry as a result of "These Things" embraced and put into practice. Every follower of Jesus is a disciple maker. Every church should embrace the calling of making disciples. This book will be a valuable tool for your spiritual growth and equip you to help others understand the fundamentals of our faith to become devoted followers of Jesus.

      — Reverend John Van Pay
      Founding and Lead Pastor of Gateway Fellowship Church

Preface

When I first met Jesus I was a sophomore in college studying psychology. At that same time I began to apprentice as a carpenter under a good friend who taught me how to use tools and let me in on the tasks of what it took to build things. One job in particular, out in the rolling countryside of East Texas, lasted for almost a year. The objective was to build a barn. But it wasn't just any barn. We milled the trees to build it right off the property and when it was finished, the big timber structure was four stories tall. It was absolutely beautiful. It won some awards. But when we began the project, there was no way to foresee that it would become through the lens of my limited experience.

First day on the job, I was ready to grab some power tools and start sawing! My friend quickly showed me that we couldn't begin anything until we worked to pour the foundation. Right. A strong foundation is profoundly important – everything rests on it. During this season, we spent several nights a week out there under the stars and my hunger to understand the things of God grew as I read his Word over and over. Though my fingers hurt each night from missing nails with the hammer and my body ached from loading boards, little did I know that as I turned the pages, I was laying a spiritual foundation for my life by letting God's Word, The Bible, take root in my heart.

As the project grew, I slowly learned how to use the most basic tools. A hammer, a handsaw, a tape measure, a trashcan (yes, that is a tool!). I was underwhelmed at my progress and looked longingly toward the chop saw and the hammer drill. However, I learned quickly that I needed a fundamental understanding of the simple tools, before I started to get my hands on the bigger stuff. I will always be grateful for the time my friend took to give me the experience I now have with carpentry years later. It has become useful in my life over and over. Comparatively, the spiritual tools that I learned to wield grew in much the same way. Just as I had slowly learned to use the various tools a carpenter needs to get the job done, I realized that there were many scholars and thinkers who had gone before me and could help me develop the spiritual tools I needed to be a lifelong disciple of Christ. Nothing has impacted my faith and changed my life more than when mature believers consistently and deliberately poured these great truths into my life. I am indebted to the men and women of God who have invested in my walk for eternity. *These Things* is a compilation of the integral truths of the discipleship process that I had the privilege to receive and in time, share with others.

A great friend and mentor once told me that "All truth is God's truth." Simply put, this book is a practical reference manual to help small group and church group leaders teach the fundamentals of Christianity in a relational, discipleship context. In this way we can pick up tools that will ultimately help us build the Church.

These Things is a compilation of countless hours of study given by many great men and women of God. We have the privilege of enjoying these great truths together, because of their hard work and dedication. I've done nothing except compile the wisdom and treasures from saints that I have read over the years and found useful in the study of these topics. My desire and hope for this work is to help prepare followers of Jesus for the work of the ministry, that the servants of God may be fully equipped for every good work (2 Timothy 3:17). These great truths and ideas are not my own, but spiritual tools to add to your belt as Paul the Apostle stated, "I delivered to you first of all that which I also received" (1 Corinthians 15:3). Each chapter begins with a brief introduction of the topic, and then follows with: 1. Supporting scriptures 2. Substantiating quotations from Christian authors 3. A short list of maxims to aid in grasping the chapter concept 4. Questions for group discussion 5. Practical challenges for further growth 6. A list of books for supplementary study specific to each topic.

The harvest truly is plentiful but the laborers are few. The greatest need in our hour is for mature and fully equipped disciples of Jesus. As scripture says, the field is "ripe and ready" for men and women of God to live out and pass on the great truths of the Christian faith, but we need more workers (Matthew 9:37). The church must once again be obedient to the commission of Christ to make disciples. An honest reflection on why the church as a whole does not fulfill this commission is that they do not know how, or the requirements for discipleship are too costly. We must rekindle the flame of devotion to service to Christ and master once again Jesus's method of discipleship.

The design on the cover is that of two great horses working the plow in the field preparing the soil for sowing and eventually, the harvest. The key to the harvest is not more sophistication of harvesting techniques but rather for more workers. More laborers in the Lord's harvest will come only when we win them, train, and equip them. If we are to win the world to Christ, it will be because each one of us has taken spiritual responsibility for others and trained them to do the same. Discipleship is ultimately taking responsibility to what is close to the heart of God, and that is people. We must not shirk from this great commission and task due to difficulty or discouragement. We must have faith that discipleship is the way of the King. Jesus says "No one, having put his hand to the plow, and looking back, is fit for the kingdom of God" (Luke 9:62). May this book be a platform of study as you grow in the Lord upon the solid foundation of his Word. I pray it leads to a life of study, learning, and humble servant hood as we strive to model the life of Jesus here on earth until we meet him face to face. Just as I had no way to perceive how remarkable the barn would become, there is no way to measure the beauty and effectiveness of a life fully yielded to Christ. Together, as we follow the King, may we pick up these tools and not look back. "And we are His witnesses to *these things*, and *so* also *is* the Holy Spirit whom God has given to those who obey Him," (Acts 5:32).

- William Kyle Volkmer

CHAPTER 1: LIFE OF JESUS

The central figure of history itself, Jesus of Nazareth, has been and ever shall be the pinnacle of humanity. Millions have found peace and intimacy with God through his life and cross. This is the story of stories; this is the Gospel.

Over two thousand years ago, God became a man in time and history in a small Roman-occupied city called Bethlehem. The God-child born at that time was not conceived by natural means but by the Holy Spirit and was born of a virgin, just as angels had announced. Jesus was God in the flesh, divinity sheathed in humanity, fully God and fully man, a walking representation of God for us. The Old Testament prophets foretold many things concerning Jesus, and one thing stands out, written by Isaiah, *"Say to those who are fearful-hearted, "Be strong, do not fear! Behold, your God will come with vengeance, With the recompense of God; He will come and save you"*(35:4).

Scriptures

Concerning The Incarnation of Jesus

John 1:1–5

> "In the beginning was the Word, and the Word was with God, and the Word was God. He was in the beginning with God. All things were made through Him, and without Him nothing was made that was made. In Him was life, and the life was the light of men. And the light shines in the darkness, and the darkness did not comprehend it."

Luke 2:11–14

> "For there is born to you this day in the city of David a Savior, who is Christ the Lord. "And this will be the sign to you: You will find a Babe wrapped in swaddling cloths, lying in a manger." And suddenly there was with the angel a multitude of the heavenly host praising God and saying: "Glory to God in the highest, And on earth peace, goodwill toward men!"

Isaiah 35:1–10

"The wilderness and the wasteland shall be glad for them, And the desert shall rejoice and blossom as the rose; It shall blossom abundantly and rejoice, Even with joy and singing. The glory of Lebanon shall be given to it, The excellence of Carmel and Sharon. They shall see the glory of the LORD, The excellency of our God. Strengthen the weak hands, And make firm the feeble knees. Say to those who are fearful-hearted, "Be strong, do not fear! Behold, your God will come with vengeance, With the recompense of God; He will come and save you." Then the eyes of the blind shall be opened, And the ears of the deaf shall be unstopped. Then the lame shall leap like a deer, And the tongue of the dumb sing. For waters shall burst forth in the wilderness, And streams in the desert. The parched ground shall become a pool, And the thirsty land springs of water; In the habitation of jackals, where each lay, There shall be grass with reeds and rushes. A highway shall be there, and a road, And it shall be called the Highway of Holiness. The unclean shall not pass over it, But it shall be for others. Whoever walks the road, although a fool, Shall not go astray. No lion shall be there, Nor shall any ravenous beast go up on it; It shall not be found there. But the redeemed shall walk there, And the ransomed of the LORD shall return, And come to Zion with singing, With everlasting joy on their heads. They shall obtain joy and gladness, And sorrow and sighing shall flee away."

Isaiah 9:6–7

"For unto us a Child is born, Unto us a Son is given; And the government will be upon His shoulder. And His name will be called Wonderful, Counselor, Mighty God, Everlasting Father, Prince of Peace. Of the increase of His government and peace There will be no end, Upon the throne of David and over His kingdom, To order it and establish it with judgment and justice From that time forward, even forever. The zeal of the LORD of hosts will perform this."

The Person and Character of Jesus of Nazareth

Loving and Gracious

Luke 18:16

"But Jesus called them to and said, "Let the little children come to Me, and do not forbid them; for of such is the kingdom of God.""

Mark 10:21

"Then Jesus, looking at him, loved him, and said to him, "One thing you lack: Go your way, sell whatever you have and give to the poor, and you will have treasure in heaven; and come, take up the cross, and follow Me.""

Eternal Existence and Historical Reference

Luke 1:1-2

"Inasmuch as many have taken in hand to set in order a narrative of those things which have been fulfilled among us, just as those who from the beginning were eyewitnesses and ministers of the word delivered them to us."

1 John 1:1–3

"That which was from the beginning, which we have heard, which we have seen with our eyes, which we have looked upon, and our hands have handled, concerning the Word of life-- the life was manifested, and we have seen, and bear witness, and declare to you that eternal life which was with the Father and was manifested to us-- that which we have seen and heard we declare to you, that you also may have fellowship with us; and truly our fellowship is with the Father and with His Son Jesus Christ."

Guiltless and Innocent Before His Accusers

John 8:46

"Which of you convicts Me of sin? And if I tell the truth, why do you not believe Me?"

Luke 23:4

"So Pilate said to the chief priests and the crowd, "I find no fault in this Man."

Full of Grace and Truth

John 1:17

"For the law was given through Moses, but grace and truth came through Jesus Christ."

John 8:4–7

Woman caught in adultery:

"They said to Him, "Teacher, this woman was caught in adultery, in the very act. "Now Moses, in the law, commanded us that such should be stoned. But what do You say?" This they said, testing Him, that they might have something of which to accuse Him. But Jesus stooped down and wrote on the ground with His finger, as though He did not hear. So when they continued asking Him, He raised Himself up and said to them, "He who is without sin among you, let him throw a stone at her first. And again He stooped down and wrote on the ground. Then those who heard it, being convicted by their conscience, went out one by one, beginning with the oldest even to the last. And Jesus was left alone, and the woman standing in the midst. When Jesus had raised Himself up and saw no one but the woman, He said to her, "Woman, where are those accusers of yours? Has no one condemned you?" She said, "No one, Lord." And Jesus said to her, "Neither do I condemn you; go and sin no more."

John 2:1–11

His first miracle:

"On the third day there was a wedding in Cana of Galilee, and the mother of Jesus was there. Now both Jesus and His disciples were invited to the wedding. And when they ran out of wine, the mother of Jesus said to Him, "They have no wine." Jesus said to her, "Woman, what does your concern have to do with Me? My hour has not yet come." His mother said to the servants, "Whatever He says to you, do it." Now there were set there six waterpots of stone, according to the manner of purification of the Jews, containing twenty or thirty gallons apiece. Jesus said to them, "Fill the waterpots with water." And they filled them up to the brim. And He said to them, "Draw some out now, and take it to the master of the feast." And they took it. When the master of the feast had tasted the water that was made wine, and did not know where it came from (but the servants who had drawn the water knew), the master of the feast called the bridegroom. And he said to him, "Every man at the beginning sets out the good wine, and when the guests have well drunk, then the inferior. You have kept the good wine until now!" This beginning of signs Jesus did in Cana of Galilee, and manifested His glory; and His disciples believed in Him."

He is Fully God and Fully Man

Colossians 2:9
> "For in Him dwells all the fullness of the Godhead bodily."

John 20:28
> "And Thomas answered and said to Him, "My Lord and my God!""

Matthew 1:21–23
> "And she will bring forth a Son, and you shall call His name JESUS, for He will save His people from their sins." So all this was done that it might be fulfilled which was spoken by the Lord through the prophet, saying: "Behold, the virgin shall be with child, and bear a Son, and they shall call His name Immanuel," which is translated, "God with us."

John 1:14

> "And the Word became flesh and dwelt among us, and we beheld His glory, the glory as of the only begotten of the Father, full of grace and truth."

John 6:57

> "As the living Father sent Me, and I live because of the Father, so he who feeds on Me will live because of Me."

Galatians 4:4

> "But when the fullness of the time had come, God sent forth His Son, born of a woman, born under the law."

Purposes of Christ

Luke 19:10
Seek and save the lost:

> "For the Son of Man has come to seek and to save that which was lost."

1 John 3:8
To destroy the works of the devil:

> "He who sins is of the devil, for the devil has sinned from the beginning. For this purpose the Son of God was manifested, that He might destroy the works of the devil."

John 6:38
To do the will of him who sent him:

> "For I have come down from heaven, not to do My own will, but the will of Him who sent Me."

Mark 10:45
To serve:

> "For even the Son of Man did not come to be served, but to serve, and to give His life a ransom for many."

John 6:40
To save:
> "And this is the will of Him who sent Me, that everyone who sees the Son and believes in Him may have everlasting life; and I will raise him up at the last day."

The Power of Christ

Power Over the Physical

Mark 6:37–44
Feeding the 5,000:
> "But He answered and said to them, "You give them something to eat." And they said to Him, "Shall we go and buy two hundred denarii worth of bread and give them something to eat?" But He said to them, "How many loaves do you have? Go and see." And when they found out they said, "Five, and two fish." Then He commanded them to make them all sit down in groups on the green grass. So they sat down in ranks, in hundreds and in fifties. And when He had taken the five loaves and the two fish, He looked up to heaven, blessed and broke the loaves, and gave them to His disciples to set before them; and the two fish He divided among them all. So they all ate and were filled. And they took up twelve baskets full of fragments and of the fish. Now those who had eaten the loaves were about five thousand men."

Luke 5:1–11
Miracle of the first catch of fish:
> "So it was, as the multitude pressed about Him to hear the word of God, that He stood by the Lake of Gennesaret, and saw two boats standing by the lake; but the fishermen had gone from them and were washing their nets. Then He got into one of the boats, which was Simon's, and asked him to put out a little from the land. And He sat down and taught the multitudes from the boat. When He had stopped speaking, He said to Simon, "Launch out into the deep and let down your nets for a catch." But Simon answered and said to Him,

"Master, we have toiled all night and caught nothing; nevertheless at Your word I will let down the net." And when they had done this, they caught a great number of fish, and their net was breaking. So they signaled to their partners in the other boat to come and help them. And they came and filled both the boats, so that they began to sink. When Simon Peter saw it, he fell down at Jesus' knees, saying, "Depart from me, for I am a sinful man, O Lord!" For he and all who were with him were astonished at the catch of fish which they had taken; and so also were James and John, the sons of Zebedee, who were partners with Simon. And Jesus said to Simon, "Do not be afraid. From now on you will catch men." So when they had brought their boats to land, they forsook all and followed Him."

Matthew 8:23–27
Calms the storm:

"And when he was entered into a ship, his disciples followed him. And, behold, there arose a great tempest in the sea, insomuch that the ship was covered with the waves: but he was asleep. And his disciples came to him, and awoke him, saying, Lord, save us: we perish. And he saith unto them, Why are ye fearful, O ye of little faith? Then he arose, and rebuked the winds and the sea; and there was a great calm. But the men marvelled, saying, What manner of man is this, that even the winds and the sea obey him!"

Power over Sickness
Isaiah 61:1–2

"The Spirit of the Lord GOD is upon Me, Because the LORD has anointed Me To preach good tidings to the poor; He has sent Me to heal the brokenhearted, To proclaim liberty to the captives, And the opening of the prison to those who are bound; To proclaim the acceptable year of the LORD, And the day of vengeance of our God; To comfort all who mourn."

Chapter 1: Life of Jesus

Matthew 4:23

"And Jesus went about all Galilee, teaching in their synagogues, preaching the gospel of the kingdom, and healing all kinds of sickness and all kinds of disease among the people."

Power over the Spiritual Realm

Matthew 11:5

"The blind see and the lame walk; the lepers are cleansed and the deaf hear; the dead are raised up and the poor have the gospel preached to them."

Matthew 10:7–8

"And as you go, preach, saying, 'The kingdom of heaven is at hand.' Heal the sick, cleanse the lepers, raise the dead, cast out demons. Freely you have received, freely give."

Death, burial, and resurrection:

Matthew 26:2

"You know that after two days is the Passover, and the Son of Man will be delivered up to be crucified."

John 2:19

"Jesus answered and said to them, "Destroy this temple, and in three days I will raise it up."

Matthew 28:6

"He is not here; for He is risen, as He said. Come, see the place where the Lord lay."

Mark 16:6

"But he said to them, "Do not be alarmed. You seek Jesus of Nazareth, who was crucified. He is risen! He is not here. See the place where they laid Him."

John 14:19
> "A little while longer and the world will see Me no more, but you will see Me. Because I live, you will live also."

Quotes

"Jesus wrote no autobiography. He left nothing in writing at all. He committed himself and his teaching simply to the hearts and memories of the men who knew and loved him. And they did not fail him. The four little books that we call Gospels are our primary and practically our only sources of information about the life and the words that have changed the world. We may wish the story has been told with greater fullness and detail; but we know that, short as it is, it is enough. And it has given Christ to every race and age."

— James S. Stewart

"Jesus was God spelling himself out in language humanity could understand."

— S.D. Gordon

"Without the way, there is no going; without the truth, there is no knowing; without the life, there is no living."

— Thomas à Kempis

"God had an only Son, and he made him a missionary."

— David Livingstone

"Whatever subject I preach, I do not stop until I reach the Savior, the Lord Jesus, for in Him are all things."

— Charles Haddon Spurgeon

"Remember that vision on the Mount of Transfiguration; and let it be ours, even in the glare of earthly joys and brightnesses, to lift up our eyes, like those wondering three, and see no man any more, save Jesus only."

— Alexander MacLaren

"The man or woman who does not know God demands an infinite satisfaction from other human beings which they cannot give, and in the case of the man, he becomes tyrannical and cruel. It springs from this one thing, the human heart must have satisfaction, but there is only one Being who can satisfy the last abyss of the human heart, and that is the Lord Jesus Christ."

— Oswald Chambers

"It is not the thinker who is the true king of men, as we sometimes hear it proudly said. We need one who will not only show, but be the Truth; who will not only point, but open and be the way; who will not only communicate thought, but give, because He is the Life. Not the rabbi's pulpit, nor the teacher's desk, still less the gilded chairs of earthly monarchs, least of all the tents of conquerors, are the throne of the true king. He rules from the cross."

— Alexander MacLaren

"You will never find Jesus so precious as when the world is one vast howling wilderness. Then he is like a rose blooming in the midst of the desolation, a rock rising above the storm."

— Robert Murray McCheyne

"I am not a Christian because God changed my life; I am a Christian because of my convictions about who Jesus Christ is."

— Josh McDowell

Maxims

- What Christ does flows from who he is; his work is an extension of his character.
- Nothing is more important to a Christian than a systematic, thorough study of the life and teachings of Jesus of Nazareth.
- One could gain incalculable wisdom from putting this book down and picking up the gospels and reading them twenty times.

Discussion Questions

1) What makes Jesus unique compared to other religious leaders?
2) What is unique regarding the Gospel?
3) Where does the power of Jesus come from?

Practical Challenges

1) Read an entire Gospel (Matthew, Mark, Luke, or John).
2) Watch the Jesus Film on YouTube. (Watch it with a friend.)

Further Study

Jesus Among Other Gods, Ravi Zacharias
The Great Physician, G. Campbell Morgan
The Gospel According to Matthew, G. Campbell Morgan
The Gospel According to Mark, G. Campbell Morgan
The Gospel According to Luke, G. Campbell Morgan
The Gospel According to John, G. Campbell Morgan
The Life of Christ, James Stalker
The Life of Lives, F.W. Farrar
The Jesus Film (YouTube)
More than a Carpenter, Josh McDowell
The Life and Times of Jesus the Messiah, Alfred Edersheim
The Life and Teaching of Jesus Christ, James S. Stewart
The Strong Name, James S. Stewart
Getting to Know Jesus, George MacDonald
The Incomparable Christ, J. Oswald Sanders

CHAPTER 2: TEACHINGS OF CHRIST

The sermons, parables, and teachings of Christ hold an unsurpassable place in history. Jesus expounded the reality of God's kingdom, the heart of the Father, the submission of the Son, the ministry of the Spirit, and finally, the role of the Church. The power behind the teachings of Christ was that they were consistent with his character and life. The eternal teachings of the Son ring true today: *"It is the Spirit who gives life; the flesh profits nothing. The words that I speak to you are spirit, and they are life."* (John 6:63).

The following claims place the listener into a valley of decision. They also make the possibility of Jesus of Nazareth being simply a good moral teacher impossible. They leave little room for interpretation but are exclusively clear regarding his character and mission. Jesus makes this crystal clear, polarizing statement, *"Therefore I said to you that you will die in your sins; for if you do not believe that I am He, you will die in your sins."* (John 8:24).

Scriptures

The Claims of Christ

Matthew 16:13–19

Jesus accepts the revelation that he is the Christ:

> "When Jesus came into the region of Caesarea Philippi, He asked His disciples, saying, "Who do men say that I, the Son of Man, am?" So they said, "Some say John the Baptist, some Elijah, and others Jeremiah or one of the prophets." He said to them, "But who do you say that I am?" Simon Peter answered and said, "You are the Christ, the Son of the living God." Jesus answered and said to him, "Blessed are you, Simon Bar-Jonah, for flesh and blood has not revealed this to you, but My Father who is in heaven. "And I also say to you that you are Peter, and on this rock I will build My church, and the gates of Hades shall not prevail against it. "And I will give you the

keys of the kingdom of heaven, and whatever you bind on earth will be bound in heaven, and whatever you loose on earth will be loosed in heaven."

John 14:6

"Jesus said to him, "I am the way, the truth, and the life. No one comes to the Father except through Me."

John 8:24

"Therefore I said to you that you will die in your sins; for if you do not believe that I am He, you will die in your sins."

John 3:18

"He who believes in Him is not condemned; but he who does not believe is condemned already, because he has not believed in the name of the only begotten Son of God."

Luke 13:3

"I tell you, no; but unless you repent you will all likewise perish."

John 11:25–26

"Jesus said to her, "I am the resurrection and the life. He who believes in Me, though he may die, he shall live. "And whoever lives and believes in Me shall never die. Do you believe this?"

John 15:1

"I am the true vine, and My Father is the vinedresser."

John 10:9

"I am the door. If anyone enters by Me, he will be saved, and will go in and out and find pasture."

John 10:11

"I am the good shepherd. The good shepherd gives His life for the sheep."

John 10:30
> "I and My Father are one."

Mark 9:37
> "Whoever receives one of these little children in My name receives Me; and whoever receives Me, receives not Me but Him who sent Me."

John 8:58
> "Jesus said to them, "Most assuredly, I say to you, before Abraham was, I AM."

Teaching Concerning the Father

The submission of the Son to the Father is the great story of loyalty and trust found within the sacred pages of scripture. Even from childhood, Jesus was about his *Father's business* (Luke 2:49). This sole desire and affection was compelled and constrained into a life of perfect love and devotion. All of his life exemplified the purpose of revealing the Father and nothing more. Watch for the words of Christ in the Gospels as in many ways he says, *"I only do what I see my Father doing…I only say what I hear my Father saying, I must be about my father's business."*

John 17:25
> "O righteous Father! The world has not known You, but I have known You; and these have known that You sent Me."

Luke 2:49
> "And He said to them, "Why did you seek Me? Did you not know that I must be about My Father's business?"

John 12:49
> "For I have not spoken on My own authority; but the Father who sent Me gave Me a command, what I should say and what I should speak."

John 5:19

> "Then Jesus answered and said to them, "Most assuredly, I say to you, the Son can do nothing of Himself, but what He sees the Father do; for whatever He does, the Son also does in like manner.""

Teaching Concerning Himself

Like the blooming of a rosebud to its full glory, we see the slow, progressive revelation of the person of Christ in the Gospel. When we look at his historical narrative and begin to hear the sermons of Christ and his powerful words, when we discern the truth of his parables and the wisdom of his warnings, the bud begins to open. Then the miraculous wonders of the hands of Jesus appear, healing and restoring all within their gentle grasp, acting as an affirmation and testimony to the truth of his teaching. Yet the greatest affirmation and validation to the message and ministry of Jesus is that God raised him from the dead. The resurrection is the stamp of God's approval on the ministry and teachings of Jesus of Nazareth.

John 3:36

> "He who believes in the Son has everlasting life; and he who does not believe the Son shall not see life, but the wrath of God abides on him."

John 12:32

> "And I, if I am lifted up from the earth, will draw all peoples to Myself."

John 17:3

> "And this is eternal life, that they may know You, the only true God, and Jesus Christ whom You have sent."

Teaching Concerning the Spirit that Has Come

I have often pondered this perplexing statement given by the Master to his disciples, *"It is to your advantage that I go away"* (John 16:7). Their question, as well as mine, is how is it good for the Master to leave us? His answer shows the brilliance of the wisdom of God in sending the Spirit, the Comforter, and the very Promise of the Father. The scope of ministry by the Spirit is not limited to location and physics and is able to simultaneously minister to millions of hearts across the globe.

John 14:26

> "But the Helper, the Holy Spirit, whom the Father will send in My name, He will teach you all things, and bring to your remembrance all things that I said to you."

Luke 24:49

> "Behold, I send the Promise of My Father upon you; but tarry in the city of Jerusalem until you are endued with power from on high."

John 15:26

> "But when the Helper comes, whom I shall send to you from the Father, the Spirit of truth who proceeds from the Father, He will testify of Me."

John 7:38–39

> "He who believes in Me, as the Scripture has said, out of his heart will flow rivers of living water." But this He spoke concerning the Spirit, whom those believing in Him would receive; for the Holy Spirit was not yet given, because Jesus was not yet glorified."

Teaching Concerning His Imminent Return

With the same confidence that we have in the truth that Jesus will save our souls and that he rose from the grave, we must trust in his imminent return. All of creation awaits this, history has marched toward it, and it is the blessed hope of the church. The justice of God demands that the nations of wicked men who mock his law shall receive the great restitution of all things.

John 14:3

"And if I go and prepare a place for you, I will come again and receive you to Myself; that where I am, there you may be also."

Luke 12:40

"Therefore you also be ready, for the Son of Man is coming at an hour you do not expect."

Matthew 24:42–44

"Watch therefore, for you do not know what hour your Lord is coming. "But know this, that if the master of the house had known what hour the thief would come, he would have watched and not allowed his house to be broken into. "Therefore you also be ready, for the Son of Man is coming at an hour you do not expect."

Quotes

"You can shut him up for a fool, you can spit at him and kill him as a demon; or you can fall at his feet and call him Lord and God. But let us not come up with any patronizing nonsense about his being a great human teacher. He has not left that open to us. He did not intend to."

— C.S. Lewis

"Not only do we not know God except through Jesus Christ; We do not even know ourselves except through Jesus Christ."

— Blaise Pascal

"Fundamentally, our Lord's message was Himself. He did not come merely to preach a Gospel; He himself is that Gospel. He did not come merely to give bread; He said, 'I am the bread.' He did not come merely to shed light; He said, 'I am the light.' He did not come merely to show the door; He said, 'I am the door.' He did not come merely to name a shepherd; He said, 'I am the shepherd.' He did not come merely to point the way; He said, 'I am the way, the truth, and the life."

— J. Sidlow Baxter

"No one else holds or has held the place in the heart of the world which Jesus holds. Other gods have been as devoutly worshipped; no other man has been so devoutly loved."

— John Knox

"We may note in passing that He was never regarded as a mere moral teacher. He did not produce that effect on any of the people who actually met Him. He produced mainly three results – Hatred –Terror – Adoration. There was no trace of people expressing mild admiration."

— C.S. Lewis

"Apart from Jesus Christ, I know little of God."

— E. Stanley Jones

"Christians believe that Jesus Christ is the son of God because He said so."

— C.S. Lewis

"As he came among men he did not try to prove the existence of God—he brought him. He lived in God and men looking upon his face could not find it within themselves to doubt God. He did not argue as Socrates, the immortality of the soul—he raised the dead. He did not speculate on how God was a Trinity—he said 'if I by the Spirit of God cast out devils, the Kingdom of God is come nigh unto you'. Here the Trinity—'I,' 'Spirit of God,' 'God'—was not something to be speculated about but was a working force for redemption—the casting out of devils and bringing in of the Kingdom. He did not teach in a didactic way about the worth of children—he put his hands upon them and setting one in their midst said 'of such is the Kingdom of God,' and he raised them from the dead. He did not argue that God answers prayer—he prayed sometimes all night and in the morning 'the power of the Lord was present to heal.' He did not paint in glowing colors the beauties of friendship and the need for human Sympathy—he wept at the grave of his friend. He did not argue the worth of womanhood and the necessity for giving them equal rights—he treated them with infinite respect, gave to them his most sublime teaching, and when he arose from the dead he appeared first to a woman. He did not teach in a schoolroom manner the necessity of humility—he 'girded himself with a towel and washed his disciples feet.' He did not discuss the question of the worth of personality as we do today—he loved and served persons. He did not discourse on the equal worth of personality—he went to the poor and outcast and ate with them. He did not prove how pain and sorrow in the universe could be compatible with the love of God—he took on himself at the cross everything that spoke against the love of God and through that pain and tragedy and sin showed the very love of God. He did not discourse on how the weakest human material can be transformed and made to contribute to the welfare of the world—he called to himself a set of weak men as the Galilean fishermen, transformed them and sent them out to begin the mightiest movement for uplift and redemption the world has ever seen. He wrote no books—only once are we told that he wrote and that was in the sand—but he wrote upon the hearts and consciences of people about him and it has become the world's most precious writing."

— E. Stanley Jones

Maxims

- Christ's claims either make him a liar, a lunatic, or the Lord.
- His claims make a claim on you.
- Jesus never asks anything of us that he wasn't willing to do.
- Jesus never said *perhaps, maybe*, or *I think so*.

Discussion Questions

1) How do we know that the teachings of Jesus are for today?
2) Why did Jesus speak in parables?
3) Does the teaching of Christ conflict with the Old Testament law?

Practical Challenges

1) Memorize the beatitudes. (Found in Matthew 5)
2) Memorize the claims of Christ. (Index cards will help)
3) Establish a Christ-first priority in your devotional reading.

Further Study

The Mind of Jesus, William Barclay
Hard Sayings of Jesus, F.F. Bruce
More Than a Carpenter, Joshua McDowell
Getting to Know Jesus, George MacDonald
Mere Christianity, C.S. Lewis
The Teaching of Christ, G. Campbell Morgan
Parables and Metaphors of Our Lord, G. Campbell Morgan
Christ of the Indian Road, E. Stanley Jones
Studies in the Sermon on the Mount, Martyn Lloyd-Jones
The Life and Teaching of Jesus Christ, James S. Stewart
Dispensational Truth, Clarence Larkin
The Life of Christ, James Stalker
The Crises of the Christ, G. Campbell Morgan
The Life of Lives, F.W. Farrar
The Strong Name, James S. Stewart
Jesus is Coming, William E. Blackstone
The Incomparable Christ, J. Oswald Sanders
Certainties of Christ's Coming, J. Oswald Sanders
The Exposition of Holy Scripture, Alexander Maclaren

CHAPTER 3: THE NATURE AND CHARACTER OF GOD

"God, who at various times and in various ways spoke in time past to the fathers by the prophets, has in these last days spoken to us by His Son, whom He has appointed heir of all things, through whom also he made the worlds; who being the brightness of His glory and the express image of His person, and upholding all things by the word of His power, when He had by Himself purged our sins, sat down at the right hand of the Majesty on high."

— Epistle to the Hebrews 1:1–3

Scriptures

God as Creator

Everything we see and cannot see was created by God. All of creation, from the outer cosmos to the bottom of the sea, declares the glory of God and the power of his spoken word. Although creation is now fallen and broken, the beauty and majesty of God's creation is still visible.

Genesis 1:1
> "In the beginning God created the heavens and the earth."

Psalm 19:1–3
> "The heavens declare the glory of God; And the firmament shows His handiwork. Day unto day utters speech, And night unto night reveals knowledge. There is no speech nor language Where their voice is not heard."

God as Holy

Inapproachably holy—if one took all the attributes and characteristics of God and orchestrated them in complementary, intensified description, one would be at the edge of the ocean regarding the holiness and awesomeness of God. It is no wonder the cherubim for eons have cried out, *"Holy, holy, holy is the Lord God almighty."*

Leviticus 10:3
> "And Moses said to Aaron, "This is what the LORD spoke, saying: 'By those who come near Me I must be regarded as holy; And before all the people I must be glorified.' " So Aaron held his peace."

Isaiah 6:3
> "And one cried to another and said: "Holy, holy, holy is the LORD of hosts; The whole earth is full of His glory!"

God as Eternal

There never was time when God was not. He has always existed and will always exist. The Hebrew conception of the name of God is the one God who was, the God who is, and the God who is to come.

Isaiah 57:15
> "For thus says the High and Lofty One Who inhabits eternity, whose name is Holy: "I dwell in the high and holy place, With him who has a contrite and humble spirit, To revive the spirit of the humble, And to revive the heart of the contrite ones."

1 Timothy 1:17
> "Now to the King eternal, immortal, invisible, to God who alone is wise, be honor and glory forever and ever. Amen."

God's Immutability

As Christians, we have confidence that there is virtue in God's character. His character, like ours, is a result of his choices. For all of time, God has chosen to be good, for the highest good for all. His throne is established in righteousness. God is choosing for righteousness, and therefore he does not change *his* standards, for it would be unwise to do so.

Malachi 3:6

> "For I am the LORD, I do not change; Therefore you are not consumed, O sons of Jacob."

Hebrews 13:8

> "Jesus Christ is the same yesterday, today and forever."

God's Omnipresence

God, as the scriptures describe him, *is* everywhere. We must, though, make the distinction that everything is not God. The ever-presence of God is to the saints a comfort and consolation, but to sinners a terror and dread.

Jeremiah 23:24

> "Can anyone hide himself in secret places, So I shall not see him?" says the LORD; "Do I not fill heaven and earth?" says the LORD. "

Acts 17:27–28

> "So that they should seek the Lord, in the hope that they might grope for Him and find Him, though He is not far from each one of us; "for in Him we live and move and have our being, as also some of your own poets have said, 'For we are also His offspring.'

God's Omniscience

Contained within the mind of God is all knowledge and wisdom. God knows everything that can be known. There is nothing in reality that is outside his intelligence.

1 Kings 8:39

> "Then hear in heaven Your dwelling place, and forgive, and act, and give to everyone according to all his ways, whose heart You know (for You alone know the hearts of all the sons of men)."

Psalm 147:5

> "Great is our Lord, and mighty in power; His understanding is infinite."

God's Omnipotence

The capacity of God's power is limitless, and yet God with this majestic power couples himself with an honest humility. As the mystics and poets have always agreed, the power of God is ultimately in the beauty of his character.

Genesis 1:1

> "In the beginning God created the heavens and the earth."

God is Light

From the first pages of creation in the account of Genesis (1:3), we hear the eternal Word echo to us this great truth, *"Let there be light."* Notice that light was not created, but rather, it was revealed from the one who dwells in unapproachable light. This same light has now brought revelation to every man in his mind and conscience.

1 John 1:5

> "This is the message which we have heard from Him and declare to you, that God is light and in Him is no darkness at all."

God is Love

This is not an ethereal concept or lofty ideal—rather, God has demonstrated a practiced disposition of unselfishness for others. The love of the Godhead is the source and pinnacle of relationships.

1 John 4:8

> "He who does not love does not know God, for God is love."

God is Spirit

The wisdom displayed on Mount Sinai teaches us that when God revealed himself on the mountain to Israel and to Moses, he reminded them again and again, that they saw no form. We are to not limit our wonder with graven form or stroke of brush. God is spirit and therefore faithfully ministers to our spirit.

John 4:24
> "God is a Spirit: and they that worship him must worship him in spirit and in truth."

The Incarnation Foretold through the Prophets

The prophets had waited and rested with hope and anticipation for the coming Savior. What a mystery of mysteries, as Isaiah prophesied that a little child would lead them.

Genesis 3:15
> "And I will put enmity Between you and the woman, And between your seed and her Seed; He shall bruise your head, And you shall bruise His heel."

Isaiah 7:14
> "Therefore the Lord Himself will give you a sign: Behold, the virgin shall conceive and bear a Son, and shall call His name Immanuel."

Isaiah 9:6–7
> "For unto us a Child is born, Unto us a Son is given; And the government will be upon His shoulder. And His name will be called Wonderful, Counselor, Mighty God, Everlasting Father, Prince of Peace. Of the increase of His government and peace There will be no end, Upon the throne of David and over His kingdom, To order it and establish it with judgment and justice From that time forward, even forever. The zeal of the LORD of hosts will perform this."

His Incarnation

The divine nature of the Son of God was perfectly united with human nature in the baby named Jesus. In the womb of a virgin, as Dr. Tozer has said, "divinity was sheathed in humanity." This is the great foundational truth of Christianity—that the Word became flesh and dwelt among us.

Colossians 2:9
>"For in Him dwells all the fullness of the Godhead bodily."

Philippians 2:6–11
>"Who, being in the form of God, did not consider it robbery to be equal with God, but made Himself of no reputation, taking the form of a bondservant, and coming in the likeness of men. And being found in appearance as a man, He humbled Himself and became obedient to the point of death, even the death of the cross. Therefore God also has highly exalted Him and given Him the name which is above every name, that at the name of Jesus every knee should bow, of those in heaven, and of those on earth, and of those under the earth, and that every tongue should confess that Jesus Christ is Lord, to the glory of God the Father."

1 Timothy 3:16
>"And without controversy great is the mystery of godliness: God was manifested in the flesh, Justified in the Spirit, Seen by angels, Preached among the Gentiles, Believed on in the world, Received up in glory."

Jesus is the Light

Men for centuries have experience the brightness of his person and the radiance of his glory. Paul expresses his worship of Jesus in this way, *"For it is the God who commanded light to shine out of darkness, who has shone in our hearts to give the light of the knowledge of the glory of God in the face of Jesus Christ."* (2 Corinthians 4:6).

John 8:12

> "Then Jesus spoke to them again, saying, "I am the light of the world. He who follows Me shall not walk in darkness, but have the light of life.""

John 1:4

> "In Him was life, and the life was the light of men."

Jesus is the Love

A love cherished within the Godhead was ultimately spread to a new community—a band of disciples on the shores of Galilee. This band was united by their newfound faith in their resurrected Messiah, and they took his message of love and self-sacrifice across the ancient world. Laying their lives down for one another, they fulfilled the commandment of their Master.

John 15:13

> "Greater love has no one than this, than to lay down one's life for his friends."

John 13:34–35

> "A new commandment I give to you, that you love one another; as I have loved you, that you also love one another. By this all will know that you are My disciples, if you have love for one another."

Jesus is the Spirit

The promise of Jesus is that he will not leave us as orphans but will come to us. The purpose of the cross of Christ is that Christ would dwell in us through the work and ministry of the Holy Spirit.

John 14:18

> "I will not leave you orphans; I will come to you."

2 Corinthians 3:17

> "Now the Lord is the Spirit; and where the Spirit of the Lord

is, there is liberty."

John 14:23
> "Jesus answered and said unto him, If a man love me, he will keep my words: and my Father will love him, and we will come unto him, and make our abode with him."

Jesus is Omnipotent

The scriptures declare that Jesus upholds all things by the word of his power (Colossians 1:17; Hebrews 1:3), that all authority in heaven and earth has been given to him, (Matthew 28:18), and that he has made a public spectacle and laughingstock of all the powers of darkness (Colossians 2:15), and yet, together with this majestic truth, he is a man of sorrows acquainted with grief (Isaiah 53:3).

Matthew 28:18
> "And Jesus came and spoke to them, saying, "All authority has been given to Me in heaven and on earth."

Matthew 19:26
> "But Jesus looked at them and said to them, "With men this is impossible, but with God all things are possible."

Jesus is Omniscient

In the days of his flesh, Jesus time and time again was able to discern the thoughts and intentions of people. Many times in the Gospels, Jesus escapes dangers, sees through deceptions, and alleviates pain.

John 16:30
> "Now we are sure that You know all things, and have no need that anyone should question You. By this we believe that You came forth from God."

John 21:17
> "He said to him the third time, "Simon, son of Jonah, do you love Me?" Peter was grieved because He said to him the third

time, "Do you love Me?" And he said to Him, "Lord, You know all things; You know that I love You." Jesus said to him, "Feed My sheep."

John 2:24–25
"But Jesus did not commit Himself to them, because He knew all men, and had no need that anyone should testify of man, for He knew what was in man."

Jesus is Omnipresent

"For where two or three are gathered together in My name, I am there in the midst of them," (Matthew 18:20). Christ is present in the churches and in the streets; there is no place to escape his presence. As poets have said long ago, *"In him we live and move and have our being."*

Matthew 28:20
"Teaching them to observe all things that I have commanded you; and lo, I am with you always, even to the end of the age." Amen.

Matthew 18:20
"For where two or three are gathered together in My name, I am there in the midst of them."

Quotes

"What comes into our minds when we think about God is the most important thing about us."

— A.W. Tozer

"The permanence of God's character guarantees the fulfillment of his promises."

— A.W. Pink

"Every once in a while in my discussions someone asks how I can believe in the Trinity. My answer is always the same. I would still be an Agnostic if there was no Trinity, because there would be no answers. Without the high order of personal unity and diversity as given in the Trinity, there are no answers."

— Francis A. Schaeffer

"Our God is the thing, or person, which we think most precious, for whom we would make the greatest sacrifice, and who moves our heart with the warmest love. He is the person or thing that if lost would leave us desolate."

— Alan Redpath

"God has communicated to man, the infinite to the finite. The one who made man capable of language in the first place has communicated to man in language about both spiritual reality and physical reality, about the nature of God and the nature of man."

— Francis A. Schaeffer

"A man rejects God neither because of intellectual demands nor because of the scarcity of evidence. A man rejects God because of a moral resistance that refuses to admit his need for God."

— Ravi Zacharias

"What were we made for? To know God. What aim should we have in life? To know God. What is the eternal life that Jesus gives? To know God. What is the best thing in life? To know God. What in humans gives God most pleasure? Knowledge of himself."

— J.I. Packer

"You can see God from anywhere if your mind is set to love and obey him."

— A.W. Tozer

"Our only business is to love and delight ourselves in God."

— Brother Lawrence

"We may ignore, but we can nowhere evade, the presence of God."
— C.S. Lewis

"Men come and go; leaders, teachers, thinkers speak and work for a season, and then fall silent and impotent. He abides. They die, but he lives. They are lights kindled, and, therefore, sooner or later quenched; but he is the true light from which they draw all their brightness, and he shines for evermore."
— Alexander MacLaren

"By the light of nature we see God as a God above us, by the light of the law we see him as a God against us, but by the light of the Gospel we see him as Emmanuel, God with us."
— Matthew Henry

"Only in the Trinity is there unity and diversity in the community of the Trinity!"
— Ravi Zacharias

Maxims

- If you have a high view of God, you will have a high view of man.
- God is God; I am not, and neither are you.
- Intrinsic value obligates.
- God has a right on our lives. God's right is founded in his value.
- The expulsive power of a greater affection.

Discussion Questions

1) Is God good by choice?
2) Is Jesus God? Explain with scriptural references.
3) How does creation reflect the Godhead?

Practical Challenges

1) Memorize one verse for each attribute of God.
2) Study the promises of God; pray them out loud.

Further Study

The Nature and Character of God, Winkie Pratney
What the Bible Teaches, R.A. Torrey
Knowing God, J.I. Packer
The Knowledge of the Holy, A.W. Tozer
The Attributes of God, A.W. Pink
The Secret of the Universe, Nathan R. Wood
The Living God, Richard D. Dehaan
The Character of God, David Pawson
God in Three Persons, Carl Brumback
He Is There and He Is Not Silent, Francis A. Schaeffer
Our Own God, G.D. Watson
The Strong Name, James S. Stewart
The Suffering of God, Terence E. Fretheim
Can Man Live without God, Ravi Zacharias
Naves Topical Bible, Orville J. Nave
All the Promises of the Bible, Herbert Lockyer
All about God in Christ in the Bible, Herbert Lockyer
All the Divine Names and Titles in the Bible, Herbert Lockyer

CHAPTER 4: THE FEAR OF THE LORD

Nothing is more desperately needed in this time and hour than to have a supernatural revelation of the fear of the Lord. The church as a whole is blind, naked, miserable, and poor. This is undoubtedly due to irreverence toward the holiness of God. The fear of the Lord is the beginning of knowledge and wisdom, the precursor and foundation of our faith, a fountain of riches, honor and life, and it is the everlasting Gospel.

Scriptures

Proverbs 1:7

> "The fear of the LORD is the beginning of knowledge, But fools despise wisdom and instruction."

Matthew 10:28

> "And do not fear those who kill the body but cannot kill the soul. But rather fear Him who is able to destroy both soul and body in hell."

Luke 12:5

> "But I will show you whom you should fear: Fear Him who, after He has killed, has power to cast into hell; yes, I say to you, fear Him!"

Psalm 89:7

> "God is greatly to be feared in the assembly of the saints, And to be held in reverence by all those around Him."

2 Corinthians 7:1

> "Therefore, having these promises, beloved, let us cleanse ourselves from all filthiness of the flesh and spirit, perfecting holiness in the fear of God."

Ecclesiastes 12:13

"Let us hear the conclusion of the whole matter: Fear God and keep His commandments, For this is man's all."

Proverbs 8:13

"The fear of the LORD is to hate evil; Pride and arrogance and the evil way And the perverse mouth I hate."

Psalm 103:13

"As a father pities his children, So the LORD pities those who fear Him."

Acts 9:31

"Then the churches throughout all Judea, Galilee, and Samaria had peace and were edified. And walking in the fear of the Lord and in the comfort of the Holy Spirit, they were multiplied."

Proverbs 10:27

"The fear of the LORD prolongs days, But the years of the wicked will be shortened."

Isaiah 66:1-2

"Thus says the LORD: "Heaven is My throne, And earth is My footstool. Where is the house that you will build Me? And where is the place of My rest? For all those things My hand has made, And all those things exist," Says the LORD. "But on this one will I look: On him who is poor and of a contrite spirit, And who trembles at My word.""

Exodus 20:20

"And Moses said to the people, "Do not fear; for God has come to test you, and that His fear may be before you, so that you may not sin.""

Deuteronomy 6:2

"That you may fear the LORD your God, to keep all His statutes and His commandments which I command you, you and your son and your grandson, all the days of your life, and that your days may be prolonged."

Joshua 24:14

"Now therefore, fear the LORD, serve Him in sincerity and in truth, and put away the gods which your fathers served on the other side of the River and in Egypt. Serve the LORD!"

Job 28:28

"And to man He said, 'Behold, the fear of the Lord, that is wisdom, And to depart from evil is understanding.' "

Psalm 2:11

"Serve the LORD with fear, And rejoice with trembling."

Psalm 25:12–13

"Who is the man that fears the LORD? Him shall He teach in the way He chooses. He himself shall dwell in prosperity, And his descendants shall inherit the earth."

Psalm 34:7–11

"The angel of the LORD encamps all around those who fear Him, And delivers them. Oh, taste and see that the LORD is good; Blessed is the man who trusts in Him! Oh, fear the LORD, you His saints! There is no want to those who fear Him. The young lions lack and suffer hunger; But those who seek the LORD shall not lack any good thing. Come, you children, listen to me; I will teach you the fear of the LORD."

Psalm 85:9

"Surely His salvation is near to those who fear Him, That glory may dwell in our land."

Psalm 119:63

> "I am a companion of all who fear You, And of those who keep Your precepts."

Psalm 128:1

> "Blessed is every one who fears the LORD, Who walks in His ways."

Psalm 147:11

> "The LORD takes pleasure in those who fear Him, In those who hope in His mercy."

Psalm 130:4

> "But there is forgiveness with You, That You may be feared."

Proverbs 3:7

> "Do not be wise in your own eyes; Fear the LORD and depart from evil."

Proverbs 16:6

> "In mercy and truth Atonement is provided for iniquity; And by the fear of the LORD one departs from evil."

Isaiah 33:6

> "Wisdom and knowledge will be the stability of your times, And the strength of salvation; The fear of the LORD is His treasure."

Malachi 4:2

> "But to you who fear My name The Sun of Righteousness shall arise With healing in His wings; And you shall go out And grow fat like stall-fed calves."

Philippians 2:12

> "Therefore, my beloved, as you have always obeyed, not as in my presence only, but now much more in my absence, work out your own salvation with fear and trembling."

Revelation 14:6–7

>"Then I saw another angel flying in the midst of heaven, having the everlasting gospel to preach to those who dwell on the earth--to every nation, tribe, tongue, and people-- saying with a loud voice, "Fear God and give glory to Him, for the hour of His judgment has come; and worship Him who made heaven and earth, the sea and springs of water."

Quotes

"Do you think the King of kings and Lord of lords is going to come into a place where he is not given due honor and reverence?"

— John Bevere

"Listen, when you see Jesus, you're not going to go up and say 'Hey buddy, I'm glad you died for me.' When you see Jesus you will be almost paralyzed with fear unless you have a glorified body and a glorified mind."

— Leonard Ravenhill

"God has never, in the history of mankind, allowed his name to go long offended."

— David Wilkerson

"The remarkable thing about God is that when you fear God, you fear nothing else, whereas if you do not fear God, you fear everything else."

— Oswald Chambers

"When men no longer fear God, they transgress his laws without hesitation. The fear of consequences is no deterrent when the fear of God is gone."

— A.W. Tozer

"In order to the attaining of all useful knowledge this is most necessary, that we fear God; we are not qualified to profit by the instructions that are given us unless our minds be possessed with a holy reverence of God, and every thought within us be brought into obedience to him…as all our knowledge must take rise from the fear of God, so it must tend to it as its perfection and center. Those know enough who know how to fear God, who are careful in everything to please him and fearful of offending him in anything; this is the alpha and omega of knowledge."

— Matthew Henry

"The fear of God is a great purifier, 'the fear of the Lord is pure.' in its own nature it is pure; in its operation it is effective. The heart is the 'temple of God;' and holy fear sweeps and purifies this temple, that it be not denied."

— Thomas Watson

"We fear men so much, because we fear God so little. One fear cures another. When man's terror scares you, turn your thoughts to the wrath of God."

— William Gurnall

"For if a man were to have all his sins laid to his charge, and communion with the devils, and as much wrath as the great God of heaven can inflict upon them, I say, if it were but for a time, even ten thousand years, if then it might have an end, there would be ground for comfort, and hopes of deliverance; but here is thy misery, this is thy state forever, here thou must be forever…when thou hast been in hell for as many thousand years as there are stars in the firmament or drops in the sea, or sands on the sea shore, yet thou hast to lie there forever. O this one word, ever, how will it torment thy soul!"

— John Wesley

"The wrath of God is like great waters that are dammed for the present; they increase more and more, and rise higher and higher, till an outlet is given; and the longer the stream is stopped, the more rapid and mighty is its course, when once it is let loose…if God should only withdraw his hand from the floodgate, it would immediately fly open, and the fiery floods of the fierceness and wrath of God, would rush forth with inconceivable fury, and would come upon you with omnipotent power; and if your strength were ten thousand times greater than it is…it would be nothing to withstand or endure it."

— Jonathan Edwards

Maxims

- Reverence equals respect.
- The secret of the Lord is with those who fear him: a link between reverence and intimacy.
- The fear of the Lord is the everlasting Gospel.

Discussion Questions

1) Is the fear of the Lord a New Testament idea? What does it mean to have a healthy fear of the Lord?
2) What does this scripture mean, "perfect love cast out all fear" (1 John 4:18).
3) How are holiness and the fear of the Lord linked?

Practical Challenges

1) By studying in your Bible, find ten verses on the fear of the Lord.
2) Ask an older, mature saint what it means to walk in the fear of the Lord.

Further Study

Nave's Topical Bible, Orville J. Nave
The Fear of the Lord, John Bevere
The Guilt of Sin, Charles G. Finney
The Fear of the Lord, John Bunyan
Intimate Friendship with God, Joy Dawson
Why Revival Tarries, Leonard Ravenhill
The Nature and Character of God, Winkie Pratney
The Joy of Fearing God, Jerry Bridges
Sodom Had No Bible, Leonard Ravenhill
Set the Trumpet to Thy Mouth, David Wilkerson
Your Day in Court (Last Day Ministries Track), Leonard Ravenhill

CHAPTER 5: SIN: WHAT IT IS AND WHAT IT IS NOT

Sin is always a departure from innocence and intimacy with God. The two questions that God asked of man in the garden were, *"Where are you?"* and *"What have you done?"* (Genesis 3:9, 4:10). God is still asking these questions of mankind. Only when one understands the costliness and travesty of sin does the Gospel come forth as good news. Man is guilty and must take personal responsibility for his own sin.

Scriptures

What Sin Is

Compiled from *The God They Never Knew,* by George Otis, Jr., Chapter 3.

Sin Is Calculated

"Sin is a transgression of God's moral law, the intent to live supremely for oneself at whatever the cost. It is a premeditated, calculated choice to live contrary to your original design. There is no absolute ignorance in sin."

— George Otis, Jr.

Matthew 5:27–28
> "You have heard that it was said to those of old, 'You shall not commit adultery.' "But I say to you that whoever looks at a woman to lust for her has already committed adultery with her in his heart."

Matthew 15:19
> "For out of the heart proceed evil thoughts, murders, adulteries, fornications, thefts, false witness, blasphemies."

Sin Is Cruel

"The ruthless, defiant, aggressive characteristics of sin..."
— George Otis, Jr.

Genesis 4:8–9
"Now Cain talked with Abel his brother; and it came to pass, when they were in the field, that Cain rose up against Abel his brother and killed him. Then the LORD said to Cain, "Where is Abel your brother?" He said, "I do not know. Am I my brother's keeper?""

Sin Is Corrosive

"Sin is a moral cancer and it tends to spread once it starts. It must be recognized as an extremely dangerous, highly active corrosive that eats away at human personality. The longer sin continues, the less actual control we have over our lives."
— George Otis, Jr.

Romans 6:23
"For the wages of sin is death, but the gift of God is eternal life in Christ Jesus our Lord."

Proverbs 13:15
"Good understanding gains favor, But the way of the unfaithful is hard."

Sin Is Continuous

"Sin is a choice to seek and maintain our happiness supremely in an unintelligent supposition that this is of paramount importance.

This state of sin and rebellion persist until exposed in an encounter with the cross of Christ."
— George Otis, Jr.

John 8:34
> "Jesus answered them, "Most assuredly, I say to you, whoever commits sin is a slave of sin."

Romans 8:7
> "Because the carnal mind is enmity against God; for it is not subject to the law of God, nor indeed can be."

Sin Is Captivity

"As sin carves its moral slide, each time down becomes easier and easier. We find ourselves inundated by habits."

— George Otis, Jr.

Romans 7:23
> "But I see another law in my members, warring against the law of my mind, and bringing me into captivity to the law of sin which is in my members."

Romans 6:16
> "Do you not know that to whom you present yourselves slaves to obey, you are that one's slaves whom you obey, whether of sin leading to death, or of obedience leading to righteousness?"

2 Corinthians 4:4
> "Whose minds the god of this age has blinded, who do not believe, lest the light of the gospel of the glory of Christ, who is the image of God, should shine on them."

What Sin Is Not

Compiled from *The God They Never Knew,* by George Otis, Jr., Chapter 3.

Sin Is Not A Substance

"Sin has and always will be a conscious moral choice, although the constitution of man is divinely created by God, it is influenced heavily by the world, the flesh and the Devil. Man's problem is not in his physical constitution but rather his deliberate developed sinful nature."

— George Otis, Jr.

Ezekiel 18:20
> "The soul who sins shall die. The son shall not bear the guilt of the father, nor the father bear the guilt of the son. The righteousness of the righteous shall be upon himself, and the wickedness of the wicked shall be upon himself."

Ecclesiastes 7:29
> "Truly, this only I have found: That God made man upright, But they have sought out many schemes."

Genesis 1:27
> "So God created man in His own image; in the image of God He created him; male and female He created them."

Psalm 139:14
> "I will praise You, for I am fearfully and wonderfully made; Marvelous are Your works, And that my soul knows very well."

Sin Is Not Sickness

"In an age of complete neglect for personal responsibility, theologians have unfortunately been swept up into the way of the world. Individuals are no longer wicked sinners, but are deemed as sick or ill and therefore the field of psychology has expanded at an alarming rate. These psychologists placate and pacify the hearts of a convicted conscience, and give false hope of self-deliverance."

— George Otis, Jr.

Chapter 5: Sin: What it is and What it is Not

Hebrews 4:15

> "For we do not have a High Priest who cannot sympathize with our weaknesses, but was in all points tempted as we are, yet without sin."

John 8:11

> "She said, "No one, Lord." And Jesus said to her, "Neither do I condemn you; go and sin no more."

Sin Is Not a Slip

"[Sin is a] deliberate, conscious, selfish choice, against what they [people] know to be true. A premeditated transgression where self-satisfaction is paramount, regardless to the consequences and pain inflicted."

— George Otis, Jr.

James 4:17

> "Therefore, to him who knows to do good and does not do it, to him it is sin."

Matthew 15:19

> "For out of the heart proceed evil thoughts, murders, adulteries, fornications, thefts, false witness, blasphemies."

Sin Is Not a Status Quo

The words of Paul describe the Christian life as one that has habitual victory over sin and that the mastery of sin has been defeated through the cross of Christ. We are no longer to be slaves to sin, but rather, slaves to righteousness—perfecting the love of God in our hearts through faith.

Romans 6:14

> "For sin shall not have dominion over you, for you are not under law but under grace."

1 John 2:1
> "My little children, these things I write to you, so that you may not sin. And if anyone sins, we have an Advocate with the Father, Jesus Christ the righteous."

Sin Is Not a Suggestion

Thoughts and temptations are not sins in and of themselves, for one must remember that our Lord Jesus was tempted in every way that we are and yet went without sin.

"You can't keep the birds from flying over your head, but you can prevent them from building a nest in your hair."

— Martin Luther

1 Corinthians 10:13
> "No temptation has overtaken you except such as is common to man; but God is faithful, who will not allow you to be tempted beyond what you are able, but with the temptation will also make the way of escape, that you may be able to bear it."

Hebrews 4:15–16
> "For we do not have a High Priest who cannot sympathize with our weaknesses, but was in all points tempted as we are, yet without sin. Let us therefore come boldly to the throne of grace, that we may obtain mercy and find grace to help in time of need."

Christians Are Free

From the Power of Sin

Romans 6:6
> "Knowing this, that our old man was crucified with Him, that the body of sin might be done away with, that we should no longer be slaves of sin."

Chapter 5: Sin: What it is and What it is Not

Romans 6:12

"Therefore do not let sin reign in your mortal body, that you should obey it in its lusts."

Romans 6:14

"For sin shall not have dominion over you, for you are not under law but under grace."

From the Practice of Sin

Galatians 5:19–21

"Now the works of the flesh are evident, which are: adultery, fornication, uncleanness, lewdness, idolatry, sorcery, hatred, contentions, jealousies, outbursts of wrath, selfish ambitions, dissensions, heresies, envy, murders, drunkenness, revelries, and the like; of which I tell you beforehand, just as I also told you in time past, that those who practice such things will not inherit the kingdom of God."

1 Corinthians 6:9–11

"Do you not know that the unrighteous will not inherit the kingdom of God? Do not be deceived. Neither fornicators, nor idolaters, nor adulterers, nor homosexuals, nor sodomites, nor thieves, nor covetous, nor drunkards, nor revilers, nor extortioners will inherit the kingdom of God. And such were some of you. But you were washed, but you were sanctified, but you were justified in the name of the Lord Jesus and by the Spirit of our God."

1 John 3:4

"Whoever commits sin also commits lawlessness, and sin is lawlessness."

From the Penalty of Sin

Revelation 20:11–15

"And I saw a great white throne, and him that sat on it, from whose face the earth and the heaven fled away; and there was found no place for them. And I saw the dead, small and great, stand before God; and the books were opened: and another book was opened, which is the book of life: and the dead were judged out of those things which were written in the books, according to their works. And the sea gave up the dead which were in it; and death and hell delivered up the dead which were in them: and they were judged every man according to their works. And death and hell were cast into the lake of fire. This is the second death. And whosoever was not found written in the book of life was cast into the lake of fire."

Matthew 25:41

"Then He will also say to those on the left hand, 'Depart from Me, you cursed, into the everlasting fire prepared for the devil and his angels."

Matthew 25:46

"And these will go away into everlasting punishment, but the righteous into eternal life."

Proverbs 29:1

"He who is often rebuked, and hardens his neck, Will suddenly be destroyed, and that without remedy."

Matthew 7:21–23

"Not everyone who says to Me, 'Lord, Lord,' shall enter the kingdom of heaven, but he who does the will of My Father in heaven. Many will say to Me in that day, 'Lord, Lord, have we not prophesied in Your name, cast out demons in Your name, and done many wonders in Your name?' "And then I will declare to them, 'I never knew you; depart from Me, you who practice lawlessness!"

Proverbs 13:15

"Good understanding gains favor, But the way of the unfaithful is hard."

Christians Are Soon to be Free from the Prevalence of Sin

Romans 3:23
> "For all have sinned, and come short of the glory of God."

1 John 5:19
> "We know that we are of God, and the whole world lies under the sway of the wicked one."

Revelation 21:1–8
> "Now I saw a new heaven and a new earth, for the first heaven and the first earth had passed away. Also there was no more sea. Then I, John, saw the holy city, New Jerusalem, coming down out of heaven from God, prepared as a bride adorned for her husband. And I heard a loud voice from heaven saying, "Behold, the tabernacle of God is with men, and He will dwell with them, and they shall be His people. God Himself will be with them and be their God. "And God will wipe away every tear from their eyes; there shall be no more death, nor sorrow, nor crying. There shall be no more pain, for the former things have passed away." Then He who sat on the throne said, "Behold, I make all things new." And He said to me, "Write, for these words are true and faithful." And He said to me, "It is done! I am the Alpha and the Omega, the Beginning and the End. I will give of the fountain of the water of life freely to him who thirsts. "He who overcomes shall inherit all things, and I will be his God and he shall be My son. "But the cowardly, unbelieving, abominable, murderers, sexually immoral, sorcerers, idolaters, and all liars shall have their part in the lake which burns with fire and brimstone, which is the second death."

Quotes

"The great and fundamental sin, which is at the foundation of all other sin, is unbelief."

— Charles G. Finney

"There are only two types of people in this world. Those who are dead to sin, and those who are dead in sin."

— Leonard Ravenhill

"The one thing which God hates is sin."

— Andrew Murray

"The Bible teaches that sin is forgiven when it is repented of, but never while it is persisted in."

— Charles G. Finney

"Take this rule: whatever weakens your reason, impairs the tenderness of your conscience, obscures your sense of God, or takes off your relish of spiritual things; in short, whatever increases the strength and authority of your body over your mind, that thing is sin to you, however innocent it may be in itself."

— Susanna Wesley

"All sin is a revolt against the heart and moral government of God, and brings guilt and condemnation."

— Gordon C. Olson

"Sin is never little."

— G. Campbell Morgan

"Any one form of sin persisted in is fatal to the soul."

— Charles G. Finney

"The most startling thing about sin is its power to enslave."

— Samuel Logan Brengle

"It is not necessary that every single member of the body should become useless and weak before death occurs. A weakness of, or a blow upon, the heart or the brain will suffice to bring an end to life, however strong and healthy other parts of the body may be. Thus one sin by its poisonous effect on the mind and heart is sufficient to ruin the spiritual life not of one only, but of a whole family or nation, even of the whole race. Such was the sin of Adam."

— Sadhu Sundar Singh

"The Bible tells us that holiness is perfect deliverance from sin."

— Samuel Logan Brengle

"Sin leads to more sin. Sin leads to worse sin."

— Jake Lefler

Maxims

- Why do you do the things you do, and who do you do them for?
- Sin is selfishness.
- God has called us to forsake all known sin.
- Man is capable and therefore culpable.
- A sin present is a sin unrepented of.
- The "I" must die.
- Intellectual deception follows moral rejection.
- Knowledge equals responsibility, responsibility accepted equals more light, and responsibility rejected equals guilt.
- God's laws are descriptions of reality from an infinite perspective.
- When you break a law, you break a heart.

Discussion Questions

1) What is remission of sin? (Luke 24:47, Mat 26:28)
2) What is the most costly thing in the universe?
3) What does it mean to be saved from sin?

Practical Challenges

1) Pray for thirty minutes that the Holy Spirit would convict you. (Repent and trust Jesus.)
2) Ask an honest, holy friend if there is sin in your life. (Don't make excuses; don't get mad at them.)

Further Study

The God They Never Knew, George Otis, Jr.
Youth Aflame ("Judas" Chapter), Winkie Pratney
The Guilt of Sin, Charles G. Finney
The Natural Ability of Man, Jesse Morrell
The Exceeding Sinfulness of Sin, Jeremiah Burroughs
The Truth Shall Make You Free, Gordon C. Olson
21st Century Reformation (PDF), Winkie Pratney
Sharing Your Faith, Gordon C. Olson
Grieve Not the Spirit, Jed Smock
Thayer's Greek Lexicon, Joseph Henry Thayer
The Expulsive Power of a Greater Affection, T. Chalmers

CHAPTER 6: THE CROSS AND THE RESURRECTION

For centuries, theologians have compiled great works expounding on the power and scope of the atonement. The fulfillment of the atonement through Jesus Christ was God's accomplishment to bring reconciliation to a broken and lost humanity and to overthrow and usurp all powers of darkness. Yet we are only on the very shores of this ocean. The correct mindset, in regards to the cross of Christ, is that it is always more and greater than we can imagine. It is the glory, hope, and destiny of all believers. As Paul so aptly stated, *"But God forbid that I should boast except in the cross of our Lord Jesus Christ, by whom the world has been crucified to me, and I to the world"* (Galatians 6:14).

Scriptures

Crucifixion and Resurrection Foretold by Jesus

John 10:14–18

> "I am the good shepherd; and I know My sheep, and am known by My own. "As the Father knows Me, even so I know the Father; and I lay down My life for the sheep. "And other sheep I have which are not of this fold; them also I must bring, and they will hear My voice; and there will be one flock and one shepherd. "Therefore My Father loves Me, because I lay down My life that I may take it again. "No one takes it from Me, but I lay it down of Myself. I have power to lay it down, and I have power to take it again. This command I have received from My Father."

John 11:25

> "Jesus said to her, "I am the resurrection and the life. He who believes in Me, though he may die, he shall live."

John 2:19

"Jesus answered and said to them, "Destroy this temple, and in three days I will raise it up.""

Mark 14:58

"We heard Him say, 'I will destroy this temple made with hands, and within three days I will build another made without hands.' "

Matthew 20:18–19

"Behold, we are going up to Jerusalem, and the Son of Man will be betrayed to the chief priests and to the scribes; and they will condemn Him to death, "and deliver Him to the Gentiles to mock and to scourge and to crucify. And the third day He will rise again."

Matthew 16:24–27

"Then Jesus said to His disciples, "If anyone desires to come after Me, let him deny himself, and take up his cross, and follow Me. "For whoever desires to save his life will lose it, but whoever loses his life for My sake will find it. "For what profit is it to a man if he gains the whole world, and loses his own soul? Or what will a man give in exchange for his soul? "For the Son of Man will come in the glory of His Father with His angels, and then He will reward each according to his works."

Crucifixion Foretold by the Prophets

Isaiah 53:1–12

"Who has believed our report? And to whom has the arm of the LORD been revealed? For He shall grow up before Him as a tender plant, And as a root out of dry ground. He has no form or comeliness; And when we see Him, There is no beauty that we should desire Him. He is despised and rejected by men, A Man of sorrows and acquainted with grief. And we hid, as it were, our faces from Him; He was despised, and we did not esteem Him. Surely He has borne our griefs And carried our sorrows; Yet we esteemed Him stricken, Smitten by God, and afflicted. But He was wounded for our transgressions, He was bruised for our iniquities; The chastisement for our peace was upon Him, And by His stripes we are healed. All we like sheep have gone astray; We have turned, every one, to his own way; And the LORD has laid on Him the iniquity of us all. He was oppressed and He was afflicted, Yet He opened not His mouth; He was led as a lamb to the slaughter, And as a sheep before its shearers is silent, So He opened not His mouth. He was taken from prison and from judgment, And who will declare His generation? For He was cut off from the land of the living; For the transgressions of My people He was stricken. And they made His grave with the wicked--But with the rich at His death, Because He had done no violence, Nor was any deceit in His mouth. Yet it pleased the LORD to bruise Him; He has put Him to grief. When You make His soul an offering for sin, He shall see His seed, He shall prolong His days, And the pleasure of the LORD shall prosper in His hand. He shall see the labor of His soul, and be satisfied. By His knowledge My righteous Servant shall justify many, For He shall bear their iniquities. Therefore I will divide Him a portion with the great, And He shall divide the spoil with the strong, Because He poured out His soul unto death, And He was numbered with the transgressors, And He bore the sin of many, And made intercession for the transgressors."

Psalm 22:1–31

"My God, My God, why have You forsaken Me? Why are You so far from helping Me, And from the words of My groaning? O My God, I cry in the daytime, but You do not hear; And in the night season, and am not silent. But You are holy, Enthroned in the praises of Israel. Our fathers trusted in You; They trusted, and You delivered them. They cried to You, and were delivered; They trusted in You, and were not ashamed. But I am a worm, and no man; A reproach of men, and despised by the people. All those who see Me ridicule Me;

They shoot out the lip, they shake the head, saying, "He trusted in the LORD, let Him rescue Him; Let Him deliver Him, since He delights in Him!" But You are He who took Me out of the womb; You made Me trust while on My mother's breasts. I was cast upon You from birth. From My mother's womb You have been My God. Be not far from Me, For trouble is near; For there is none to help. Many bulls have surrounded Me; Strong bulls of Bashan have encircled Me. They gape at Me with their mouths, Like a raging and roaring lion. I am poured out like water, And all My bones are out of joint; My heart is like wax; It has melted within Me. My strength is dried up like a potsherd, And My tongue clings to My jaws; You have brought Me to the dust of death. For dogs have surrounded Me; The congregation of the wicked has enclosed Me. They pierced My hands and My feet; I can count all My bones. They look and stare at Me. They divide My garments among them, And for My clothing they cast lots. But You, O LORD, do not be far from Me; O My Strength, hasten to help Me! Deliver Me from the sword, My precious life from the power of the dog. Save Me from the lion's mouth And from the horns of the wild oxen! You have answered Me. I will declare Your name to My brethren; In the midst of the assembly I will praise You. You who fear the LORD, praise Him! All you descendants of Jacob, glorify Him, And fear Him, all you offspring of Israel! For He has not despised nor abhorred the affliction of the afflicted; Nor has He hidden His face from Him; But when He cried to Him, He heard. My praise shall be of You in the great assembly; I will pay My vows before those who fear Him. The poor shall eat and be satisfied; Those who seek Him will praise the LORD. Let your heart live forever! All the ends of the world Shall remember and turn to the LORD, And all the families of the nations Shall worship before You. For the kingdom is the LORD's, And He rules over the nations. All the prosperous of the earth Shall eat and worship; All those who go down to the dust Shall bow before Him, Even he who cannot keep himself alive. A posterity shall serve Him. It will be recounted of the Lord to the next generation, They will come and declare His righteousness to a people who will be born, That He has done this."

The Crucifixion in the Gospels

Mark 15:16–20

"Then the soldiers led Him away into the hall called Praetorium, and they called together the whole garrison. And they clothed Him with purple; and they twisted a crown of thorns, put it on His head, and began to salute Him, "Hail, King of the Jews!" Then they struck Him on the head with a reed and spat on Him; and bowing the knee, they worshiped Him. And when they had mocked Him, they took the purple off Him, put His own clothes on Him, and led Him out to crucify Him."

Luke 22:63–65

"Now the men who held Jesus mocked Him and beat Him. And having blindfolded Him, they struck Him on the face and asked Him, saying, "Prophesy! Who is the one who struck You?" And many other things they blasphemously spoke against Him."

John 19:1–15

"So then Pilate took Jesus and scourged Him. And the soldiers twisted a crown of thorns and put it on His head, and they put on Him a purple robe. Then they said, "Hail, King of the Jews!" And they struck Him with their hands. Pilate then went out again, and said to them, "Behold, I am bringing Him out to you, that you may know that I find no fault in Him." Then Jesus came out, wearing the crown of thorns and the purple robe. And Pilate said to them, "Behold the Man!" Therefore, when the chief priests and officers saw Him, they cried out, saying, "Crucify Him, crucify Him!" Pilate said to them, "You take Him and crucify Him, for I find no fault in Him." The Jews answered him, "We have a law, and according to our law

He ought to die, because He made Himself the Son of God."
Therefore, when Pilate heard that saying, he was the more
afraid, and went again into the Praetorium, and said to Jesus,
"Where are You from?" But Jesus gave him no answer. Then
Pilate said to Him, "Are You not speaking to me? Do You not
know that I have power to crucify You, and power to release
You?" Jesus answered, "You could have no power at all
against Me unless it had been given you from above.
Therefore the one who delivered Me to you has the greater
sin." From then on Pilate sought to release Him, but the Jews
cried out, saying, "If you let this Man go, you are not Caesar's
friend. Whoever makes himself a king speaks against Caesar."
When Pilate therefore heard that saying, he brought Jesus out
and sat down in the judgment seat in a place that is called The
Pavement, but in Hebrew, Gabbatha. Now it was the
Preparation Day of the Passover, and about the sixth hour.
And he said to the Jews, "Behold your King!" But they cried
out, "Away with Him, away with Him! Crucify Him!" Pilate
said to them, "Shall I crucify your King?" The chief priests
answered, "We have no king but Caesar!"

Luke 23:26–43

"Now as they led Him away, they laid hold of a certain man,
Simon a Cyrenian, who was coming from the country, and on
him they laid the cross that he might bear it after Jesus. And a
great multitude of the people followed Him, and women who
also mourned and lamented Him. But Jesus, turning to them,
said, "Daughters of Jerusalem, do not weep for Me, but weep
for yourselves and for your children. "For indeed the days are
coming in which they will say, 'Blessed are the barren, wombs
that never bore, and breasts which never nursed!' "Then they
will begin 'to say to the mountains, "Fall on us!" and to the
hills, "Cover us!" ' "For if they do these things in the green
wood, what will be done in the dry?" There were also two
others, criminals, led with Him to be put to death. And when
they had come to the place called Calvary, there they crucified
Him, and the criminals, one on the right hand and the other on

the left. Then Jesus said, "Father, forgive them, for they do not know what they do." And they divided His garments and cast lots. And the people stood looking on. But even the rulers with them sneered, saying, "He saved others; let Him save Himself if He is the Christ, the chosen of God." The soldiers also mocked Him, coming and offering Him sour wine, and saying, "If You are the King of the Jews, save Yourself." And an inscription also was written over Him in letters of Greek, Latin, and Hebrew: THIS IS THE KING OF THE JEWS. Then one of the criminals who were hanged blasphemed Him, saying, "If You are the Christ, save Yourself and us." But the other, answering, rebuked him, saying, "Do you not even fear God, seeing you are under the same condemnation? "And we indeed justly, for we receive the due reward of our deeds; but this Man has done nothing wrong." Then he said to Jesus, "Lord, remember me when You come into Your kingdom." And Jesus said to him, "Assuredly, I say to you, today you will be with Me in Paradise."

John 19:16–27

"Then he delivered Him to them to be crucified. So they took Jesus and led Him away. And He, bearing His cross, went out to a place called the Place of a Skull, which is called in Hebrew, Golgotha, where they crucified Him, and two others with Him, one on either side, and Jesus in the center. Now Pilate wrote a title and put it on the cross. And the writing was: JESUS OF NAZARETH, THE KING OF THE JEWS. Then many of the Jews read this title, for the place where Jesus was crucified was near the city; and it was written in Hebrew, Greek, and Latin. Therefore the chief priests of the Jews said to Pilate, "Do not write, 'The King of the Jews,' but, 'He said, "I am the King of the Jews." ' " Pilate answered, "What I have written, I have written." Then the soldiers, when they had crucified Jesus, took His garments and made four parts, to each soldier a part, and also the tunic. Now the tunic was without seam, woven from the top in one piece. They said therefore among themselves, "Let us not tear it, but cast lots for it, whose it shall be," that the Scripture might be fulfilled which says: "They divided My garments among them, And for My clothing they cast lots." Therefore the soldiers did these things. Now there stood by the cross of Jesus His mother, and His mother's sister, Mary the wife of Clopas, and Mary Magdalene. When Jesus therefore saw His mother, and the disciple whom He loved standing by, He said to His mother, "Woman, behold your son!" Then He said to the disciple, "Behold your mother!" And from that hour that disciple took her to his own home."

Mark 15:33–41

"Now when the sixth hour had come, there was darkness over the whole land until the ninth hour. And at the ninth hour Jesus cried out with a loud voice, saying, "Eloi, Eloi, lama sabachthani?" which is translated, "My God, My God, why have You forsaken Me?" Some of those who stood by, when they heard that, said, "Look, He is calling for Elijah!" Then someone ran and filled a sponge full of sour wine, put it on a reed, and offered it to Him to drink, saying, "Let Him alone; let us see if Elijah will come to take Him down." And Jesus cried out with a loud voice, and breathed His last. Then the veil of the temple was torn in two from top to bottom. So when the centurion, who stood opposite Him, saw that He cried out like this and breathed His last, he said, "Truly this Man was the Son of God!" There were also women looking on from afar, among whom were Mary Magdalene, Mary the mother of James the Less and of Joses, and Salome, who also followed Him and ministered to Him when He was in Galilee, and many other women who came up with Him to Jerusalem."

Luke 23:44–49

"Now it was about the sixth hour, and there was darkness over all the earth until the ninth hour. Then the sun was darkened, and the veil of the temple was torn in two. And when Jesus had cried out with a loud voice, He said, "Father, 'into Your hands I commit My spirit.' " Having said this, He breathed His last. So when the centurion saw what had happened, he glorified God, saying, "Certainly this was a righteous Man!" And the whole crowd who came together to that sight, seeing what had been done, beat their breasts and returned. But all His acquaintances, and the women who followed Him from Galilee, stood at a distance, watching these things."

John 19:28–30

"After this, Jesus, knowing that all things were now accomplished, that the Scripture might be fulfilled, said, "I thirst!" Now a vessel full of sour wine was sitting there; and they filled a sponge with sour wine, put it on hyssop, and put it to His mouth. So when Jesus had received the sour wine, He said, "It is finished!" And bowing His head, He gave up His spirit."

The Burial of Jesus

Isaiah 53:9–12

"And they made His grave with the wicked--But with the rich at His death, Because He had done no violence, Nor was any deceit in His mouth. Yet it pleased the LORD to bruise Him; He has put Him to grief. When You make His soul an offering for sin, He shall see His seed, He shall prolong His days, And the pleasure of the LORD shall prosper in His hand. He shall see the labor of His soul, and be satisfied. By His knowledge My righteous Servant shall justify many, For He shall bear their iniquities. Therefore I will divide Him a portion with the great, And He shall divide the spoil with the strong, Because He poured out His soul unto death, And He was numbered with the transgressors, And He bore the sin of many, And made intercession for the transgressors."

Mark 15:42–47

"Now when evening had come, because it was the Preparation Day, that is, the day before the Sabbath, Joseph of Arimathea, a prominent council member, who was himself waiting for the kingdom of God, coming and taking courage, went in to Pilate and asked for the body of Jesus. Pilate marveled that He was already dead; and summoning the centurion, he asked him if He had been dead for some time. So when he found out from the centurion, he granted the body to Joseph. Then he bought fine linen, took Him down, and wrapped Him in the linen. And he laid Him in a tomb which had been hewn out of the rock, and rolled a stone against the door of the tomb. And Mary Magdalene and Mary the mother of Joses observed where He was laid."

Luke 23:50–56

"Now behold, there was a man named Joseph, a council member, a good and just man. He had not consented to their decision and deed. He was from Arimathea, a city of the Jews, who himself was also waiting for the kingdom of God. This man went to Pilate and asked for the body of Jesus. Then he took it down, wrapped it in linen, and laid it in a tomb that was hewn out of the rock, where no one had ever lain before. That day was the Preparation, and the Sabbath drew near. And the women who had come with Him from Galilee followed after, and they observed the tomb and how His body was laid. Then they returned and prepared spices and fragrant oils. And they rested on the Sabbath according to the commandment."

John 19:38–42

"After this, Joseph of Arimathea, being a disciple of Jesus, but secretly, for fear of the Jews, asked Pilate that he might take away the body of Jesus; and Pilate gave him permission. So he came and took the body of Jesus. And Nicodemus, who at first came to Jesus by night, also came, bringing a mixture of myrrh and aloes, about a hundred pounds. Then they took the body of Jesus, and bound it in strips of linen with the spices, as the custom of the Jews is to bury. Now in the place where He was crucified there was a garden, and in the garden a new tomb in which no one had yet been laid. So there they laid Jesus, because of the Jews' Preparation Day, for the tomb was nearby."

Matthew 27:62–66
The guard at the tomb:

> "On the next day, which followed the Day of Preparation, the
> chief priests and Pharisees gathered together to Pilate, saying,
> "Sir, we remember, while He was still alive, how that deceiver
> said, 'After three days I will rise.' "Therefore command that
> the tomb be made secure until the third day, lest His disciples
> come by night and steal Him away, and say to the people, 'He
> has risen from the dead.' So the last deception will be worse
> than the first." Pilate said to them, "You have a guard; go your
> way, make it as secure as you know how." So they went and
> made the tomb secure, sealing the stone and setting the
> guard."

The Testimony of the Resurrection

1 Corinthians 15:1–8

> "Moreover, brethren, I declare to you the gospel which I
> preached to you, which also you received and in which you
> stand, by which also you are saved, if you hold fast that word
> which I preached to you--unless you believed in vain. For I
> delivered to you first of all that which I also received: that
> Christ died for our sins according to the Scriptures, and that
> He was buried, and that He rose again the third day according
> to the Scriptures, and that He was seen by Cephas, then by the
> twelve. After that He was seen by over five hundred brethren
> at once, of whom the greater part remain to the present, but
> some have fallen asleep. After that He was seen by James,
> then by all the apostles. Then last of all He was seen by me
> also, as by one born out of due time."

Matthew 28:6

> "He is not here; for He is risen, as He said. Come, see the
> place where the Lord lay."

2 Corinthians 4:13–14

> "And since we have the same spirit of faith, according to what
> is written, "I believed and therefore I spoke," we also believe

and therefore speak, knowing that He who raised up the Lord Jesus will also raise us up with Jesus, and will present us with you."

Things to Remember Concerning the Resurrection

- Multiple eyewitness testimonies corroborate the miraculous event.
- Ancient non-Christian sources speak of Christ, Christians, and the crucifixion, and some mention a resurrection. (In *The Case for the Resurrection of Jesus*, Gary Habermas and Mike Licona list more than forty sources that mention Jesus within 150 years of his life).
- The disciples seal the validity of their testimonies by shedding their own blood (martyred for their faith).
- Historically recorded changes in character after the resurrection (Peter, Paul, etc.).
- Resurrection life and power experienced by millions of followers worldwide (the qualitative experiences of Christian believers worldwide throughout history).

Quotes

"At the cross God wrapped his heart in flesh and blood and let it be nailed to the cross for our redemption."

— E. Stanley Jones

"The bodily resurrection of Jesus Christ from the dead is the crowning proof of Christianity. If the resurrection did not take place, then Christianity is a false religion. If it did take place, then Christ is God and the Christian faith is absolute truth."

— Henry Morris

"Outside of the resurrection of Jesus, I do not know of any other hope for this world."

— Chancellor Adenauer

"God may thunder his commands from Mount Sinai and men may fear, yet remain at heart exactly as they were before. But let a man once see his God down in the arena as a man—suffering, tempted, sweating, and agonized, finally dying a criminal's death—and he is a hard man indeed who is untouched."

— J.B. Phillips

"How strange this fear of death is! We are never frightened at a sunset."

— George Macdonald

"A man who was completely innocent, offered himself as a sacrifice for the good of others, including his enemies, and became the ransom of the world. It was a perfect act."

— Mahatma Gandhi

"Every day I need the cross more…Every day I live this Christian life I am more and more conscious that I cannot understand the mystery of all Jesus did; yet more and more conscious that by the way of that cross, and that cross alone, my wounded heart is healed, my withered soul is renewed, my deformed spirit is built up, my broken manhood is remade; and every day I live I sing in my heart with new meaning."

— G. Campbell Morgan

"Christianity is the only religion whose God bears the scars of evil."

— Os Guinness

"The significance of the resurrection of Jesus lies in the fact that it is not just any old Joe Blow who has been raised from the dead, but Jesus of Nazareth, whose crucifixion was instigated by the Jewish leadership because of his blasphemous claims to divine authority. If this man has been raised from the dead, then the God whom he allegedly blasphemed has clearly vindicated his claims. Thus, in an age of religious relativism and pluralism, the resurrection of Jesus constitutes a solid rock on which Christians can take their stand for God's decisive self-revelation in Jesus."

— Dr. William Lane Craig

Maxims

- His empty tomb is your empty tomb.
- The Gospels are eyewitness testimonies.
- The cross bears those who bear it.
- The cross is heavy.
- He is risen. He is risen indeed.
- The resurrection of Jesus Christ is a historical fact.

Discussion Questions

1) Why did Jesus have to die?
2) Is the resurrection of Christ historically verifiable?
3) What are the consequences of Jesus not rising from the dead?

Practical Challenges

1) Meditate for thirty minutes on what Jesus did for us on the cross.
2) Read the above scripture verses out loud. (*Faith comes by hearing*, Romans 10:17)

Further Study

12 Sermons on the Resurrection, Charles Spurgeon
The Blood of the Cross, Andrew Murray
The God They Never Knew (Chapter 5), George Otis, Jr.
The Atonement, Albert Barnes
Resurrection Life and Power, Samuel Logan Brengle
Bread and Wine, Plough Publishing
Guest of the Soul ("Atonement" chapter), Samuel Logan Brengle
The Cross is Heaven, Sadhu Sundar Singh
The Christian After Death, Robert Ervin Hough
Christ and Human Suffering, E. Stanley Jones
Therefore Stand, Wilbur Moorehead Smith
Evidence That Demands a Verdict, Josh McDowell
Understanding the Atonement for the Mission of the Church, John Driver

CHAPTER 7 : SALVATION
Section 1: God's Part

Salvation, in its essence, is being saved from sin unto God. Salvation is twofold: God's provision through the Savior's death, burial, and resurrection, coupled with man's response of repentance, and faith in Christ Jesus. Salvation is not a work, separate and apart from Christ, but rather Christ himself imparted through faith to the believer. This divine union is Christ in you, the source, assurance, and power of salvation.

Scriptures

His Part

God has brought all things near through the blood of the cross; he has upheld the majesty of the law and kingdom and found a way through his cross to wisely forgive sins.

Matthew 1:21
> "And she will bring forth a Son, and you shall call His name JESUS, for He will save His people from their sins."

John 3:15–18
> "That whoever believes in Him should not perish but have eternal life. "For God so loved the world that He gave His only begotten Son, that whoever believes in Him should not perish but have everlasting life. "For God did not send His Son into the world to condemn the world, but that the world through Him might be saved. "He who believes in Him is not condemned; but he who does not believe is condemned already, because he has not believed in the name of the only begotten Son of God."

Romans 5:6–11
"For when we were still without strength, in due time Christ died for

the ungodly. For scarcely for a righteous man will one die; yet perhaps for a good man someone would even dare to die. But God demonstrates His own love toward us, in that while we were still sinners, Christ died for us. Much more then, having now been justified by His blood, we shall be saved from wrath through Him. For if when we were enemies we were reconciled to God through the death of His Son, much more, having been reconciled, we shall be saved by His life. And not only that, but we also rejoice in God through our Lord Jesus Christ, through whom we have now received the reconciliation."

2 Corinthians 5:20

"Now then, we are ambassadors for Christ, as though God were pleading through us: we implore you on Christ's behalf, be reconciled to God."

2 Peter 3:9

"The Lord is not slack concerning His promise, as some count slackness, but is longsuffering toward us, not willing that any should perish but that all should come to repentance."

Our Part

Our response to the sufficient provision from God's pain and sacrifice is that we turn from our sin and put our absolute trust and reliance in Jesus. We believe His death, burial, and resurrection, will lead to ours.

Acts 2:38

"Then Peter said to them, "Repent, and let every one of you be baptized in the name of Jesus Christ for the remission of sins; and you shall receive the gift of the Holy Spirit."

Hebrews 5:9

"And having been perfected, He became the author of eternal salvation to all who obey Him."

John 15:7

> "If you abide in Me, and My words abide in you, you will ask what you desire, and it shall be done for you."

Romans 10:9

> "That if you confess with your mouth the Lord Jesus and believe in your heart that God has raised Him from the dead, you will be saved."

John 17:3

> "And this is eternal life, that they may know You, the only true God, and Jesus Christ whom You have sent."

The Normal Christian Birth Contains Four Typical and Essential Elements

Then Peter said to them, "Repent, and let every one of you be baptized in the name of Jesus Christ for the remission of sins; and you shall receive the gift of the Holy Spirit."

— Acts 2:38

Repentance

To repent means to turn from your old ways—thoughts, habits, and actions. Webster's definition: to turn from sin and dedicate oneself to the amendment of one's life.

Luke 13:3

> "I tell you, no; but unless you repent you will all likewise perish."

Mark 1:5

> "Then all the land of Judea, and those from Jerusalem, went out to him and were all baptized by him in the Jordan River, confessing their sins."

2 Corinthians 7:10

"For godly sorrow produces repentance leading to salvation, not to be regretted; but the sorrow of the world produces death."

Belief and Trust in Jesus

Faith has been described as placing absolute trust and reliance on God's salvation through Jesus. This is what it means to believe in God.

Acts 16:31

"So they said, "Believe on the Lord Jesus Christ, and you will be saved, you and your household."

Romans 10:9

"That if you confess with your mouth the Lord Jesus and believe in your heart that God has raised Him from the dead, you will be saved."

Acts 4:12

"Nor is there salvation in any other, for there is no other name under heaven given among men by which we must be saved."

Baptism

Baptism in water is an outward expression of an inward surrender and transformation. It is an expression of your repentance and faith.

Matthew 28:18–19

"And Jesus came and spoke to them, saying, "All authority has been given to Me in heaven and on earth. "Go therefore and make disciples of all the nations, baptizing them in the name of the Father and of the Son and of the Holy Spirit."

Mark 16:16

"He who believes and is baptized will be saved; but he who

does not believe will be condemned."

Acts 8:36

"Now as they went down the road, they came to some water. And the eunuch said, "See, here is water. What hinders me from being baptized?"

Receiving the baptism in the Holy Spirit

In the countless normal Christian births depicted in the histories of the Acts of the Apostles, the baptism in the Holy Spirit plays an indispensable part of the believer's salvation experience. This baptism of love, makes Jesus real to you, and known to others. One should expect supernatural evidence to accompany this baptism: tongues, prophecy, and supernaturally empowered speech.

John 3:5

"Jesus answered, "Most assuredly, I say to you, unless one is born of water and the Spirit, he cannot enter the kingdom of God."

Acts 1:8

"But you shall receive power when the Holy Spirit has come upon you; and you shall be witnesses to Me in Jerusalem, and in all Judea and Samaria, and to the end of the earth."

John 7:38–39

"He who believes in Me, as the Scripture has said, out of his heart will flow rivers of living water." But this He spoke concerning the Spirit, whom those believing in Him would receive; for the Holy Spirit was not yet given, because Jesus was not yet glorified."

Indwelling Evidence of Salvation

Ephesians 3:17

"That Christ may dwell in your hearts through faith; that you, being rooted and grounded in love."

Colossians 1:27

"To them God willed to make known what are the riches of
the glory of this mystery among the Gentiles: which is Christ
in you, the hope of glory."

Romans 8:16

"The Spirit Himself bears witness with our spirit that we are
children of God."

Mark 16:17–20

"And these signs will follow those who believe: In My name
they will cast out demons; they will speak with new tongues;
"they will take up serpents; and if they drink anything deadly,
it will by no means hurt them; they will lay hands on the sick,
and they will recover." So then, after the Lord had spoken to
them, He was received up into heaven, and sat down at the
right hand of God. And they went out and preached
everywhere, the Lord working with them and confirming the
word through the accompanying signs. Amen."

Acts 26:18

"To open their eyes, in order to turn them from darkness to
light, and from the power of Satan to God, that they may
receive forgiveness of sins and an inheritance among those
who are sanctified by faith in Me."

The Visible Evidence of Salvation

The following list of "The Marks of the New Birth" was compiled by
Winkie Pratney.

Desire for Scripture

A newborn baby that is not eating is either sick or dead. An indicator
of new birth is an insatiable hunger for the very words of God. This
hunger can be developed through the discipline of reading. Blessed
are those who hunger and thirst.

Deuteronomy 6:5–7

"You shall love the LORD your God with all your heart, with all your soul, and with all your strength. "And these words which I command you today shall be in your heart. "You shall teach them diligently to your children, and shall talk of them when you sit in your house, when you walk by the way, when you lie down, and when you rise up."

Job 23:12

"I have not departed from the commandment of His lips; I have treasured the words of His mouth More than my necessary food."

Jeremiah 15:16

"Your words were found, and I ate them, And Your word was to me the joy and rejoicing of my heart; For I am called by Your name, O LORD God of hosts."

Romans 10:17

"So then faith comes by hearing, and hearing by the word of God."

1 Peter 2:2

"As newborn babes, desire the pure milk of the word, that you may grow thereby."

Difference of Standards

The old hymn says, "The things of earth will grow strangely dim in the light of His glory and grace." This indicator of new birth is a testimony to the transformative power of the gospel.

1 Corinthians 10:13

"No temptation has overtaken you except such as is common to man; but God is faithful, who will not allow you to be tempted beyond what you are able, but with the temptation will also make the way of escape, that you may be able to bear it."

Galatians 6:15–16

"For in Christ Jesus neither circumcision nor uncircumcision avails anything, but a new creation. And as many as walk according to this rule, peace and mercy be upon them, and upon the Israel of God."

Ephesians 4:20–24

"But you have not so learned Christ, if indeed you have heard Him and have been taught by Him, as the truth is in Jesus: that you put off, concerning your former conduct, the old man which grows corrupt according to the deceitful lusts, and be renewed in the spirit of your mind, and that you put on the new man which was created according to God, in true righteousness and holiness."

Philippians 3:7

"But what things were gain to me, these I have counted loss for Christ."

1 Peter 1:13–16

"Therefore gird up the loins of your mind, be sober, and rest your hope fully upon the grace that is to be brought to you at the revelation of Jesus Christ; as obedient children, not conforming yourselves to the former lusts, as in your ignorance; but as He who called you is holy, you also be holy in all your conduct, because it is written, "Be holy, for I am holy.""

1 John 3:1–3

"Behold what manner of love the Father has bestowed on us, that we should be called children of God! Therefore the world does not know us, because it did not know Him. Beloved, now we are children of God; and it has not yet been revealed what we shall be, but we know that when He is revealed, we shall be like Him, for we shall see Him as He is. And everyone who has this hope in Him purifies himself, just as He is pure."

Discipline of Self

With every great privilege there is a great responsibility. The miracle of God's salvation still fleshes itself out in a life of devotion and sacrifice. The cardinal ethic of Christianity is sacrifice.

Matthew 16:24
> "Then Jesus said to His disciples, "If anyone desires to come after Me, let him deny himself, and take up his cross, and follow Me."

Luke 3:11
> "He answered and said to them, "He who has two tunics, let him give to him who has none; and he who has food, let him do likewise."

John 15:2
> "Every branch in Me that does not bear fruit He takes away; and every branch that bears fruit He prunes, that it may bear more fruit."

1 Corinthians 9:25–27
> "And everyone who competes for the prize is temperate in all things. Now they do it to obtain a perishable crown, but we for an imperishable crown. Therefore I run thus: not with uncertainty. Thus I fight: not as one who beats the air. But I discipline my body and bring it into subjection, lest, when I have preached to others, I myself should become disqualified."

1 Corinthians 10:13
> "No temptation has overtaken you except such as is common to man; but God is faithful, who will not allow you to be tempted beyond what you are able, but with the temptation

will also make the way of escape, that you may be able to bear it."

Galatians 5:22–23

"But the fruit of the Spirit is love, joy, peace, longsuffering, kindness, goodness, faithfulness, gentleness, self-control. Against such there is no law."

1 John 4:17

"Love has been perfected among us in this: that we may have boldness in the day of judgment; because as He is, so are we in this world."

Despised by Society

Blessed are you when the world hates you and despises you, for they will never treat you any better than the way they treated him.

Matthew 5:10–12

"Blessed are those who are persecuted for righteousness' sake, For theirs is the kingdom of heaven. "Blessed are you when they revile and persecute you, and say all kinds of evil against you falsely for My sake. "Rejoice and be exceedingly glad, for great is your reward in heaven, for so they persecuted the prophets who were before you."

John 15:18–21

"If the world hates you, you know that it hated Me before it hated you. "If you were of the world, the world would love its own. Yet because you are not of the world, but I chose you out of the world, therefore the world hates you. "Remember the word that I said to you, 'A servant is not greater than his master.' If they persecuted Me, they will also persecute you. If they kept My word, they will keep yours also. "But all these things they will do to you for My name's sake, because they do not know Him who sent Me."

Romans 8:18

> "For I consider that the sufferings of this present time are not worthy to be compared with the glory which shall be revealed in us."

Romans 12:20–21

> "Therefore "If your enemy is hungry, feed him; If he is thirsty, give him a drink; For in so doing you will heap coals of fire on his head." Do not be overcome by evil, but overcome evil with good.""

2 Timothy 2:12

> "If we endure, We shall also reign with Him. If we deny Him, He also will deny us."

1 Peter 2:20–21

> "For what credit is it if, when you are beaten for your faults, you take it patiently? But when you do good and suffer, if you take it patiently, this is commendable before God. For to this you were called, because Christ also suffered for us, leaving us an example, that you should follow His steps."

Seeks Other Christians

The gospel was birthed in a community, not on isolated mountain tops, in caves, or in abbeys, but rather, the Spirit has always expressed himself fully through community.

Romans 15:5–6

> "Now may the God of patience and comfort grant you to be like-minded toward one another, according to Christ Jesus, that you may with one mind and one mouth glorify the God and Father of our Lord Jesus Christ."

Acts 2:42

> "And they continued steadfastly in the apostles' doctrine and fellowship, in the breaking of bread, and in prayers."

Ephesians 3:17–19

"That Christ may dwell in your hearts through faith; that you, being rooted and grounded in love, may be able to comprehend with all the saints what is the width and length and depth and height-- to know the love of Christ which passes knowledge; that you may be filled with all the fullness of God."

Hebrews 10:25

"Not forsaking the assembling of ourselves together, as is the manner of some, but exhorting one another, and so much the more as you see the Day approaching."

1 Peter 1:22

"Since you have purified your souls in obeying the truth through the Spirit in sincere love of the brethren, love one another fervently with a pure heart."

1 John 1:2, 7

"The life was manifested, and we have seen, and bear witness, and declare to you that eternal life which was with the Father and was manifested to us-- ... But if we walk in the light as He is in the light, we have fellowship with one another, and the blood of Jesus Christ His Son cleanses us from all sin."

1 John 3:14

"We know that we have passed from death to life, because we love the brethren. He who does not love his brother abides in death."

Serves the Lord

Let this mind be in you which was also in Christ Jesus, this mind of a servant; he came to serve, not be served. A Christian life is ultimately a life of service.

1 John 3:17

> "But whoever has this world's goods, and sees his brother in need, and shuts up his heart from him, how does the love of God abide in him?"

1 John 3:16–24

> "By this we know love, because He laid down His life for us. And we also ought to lay down our lives for the brethren. But whoever has this world's goods, and sees his brother in need, and shuts up his heart from him, how does the love of God abide in him? My little children, let us not love in word or in tongue, but in deed and in truth. And by this we know that we are of the truth, and shall assure our hearts before Him. For if our heart condemns us, God is greater than our heart, and knows all things. Beloved, if our heart does not condemn us, we have confidence toward God. And whatever we ask we receive from Him, because we keep His commandments and do those things that are pleasing in His sight. And this is His commandment: that we should believe on the name of His Son Jesus Christ and love one another, as He gave us commandment. Now he who keeps His commandments abides in Him, and He in him. And by this we know that He abides in us, by the Spirit whom He has given us."

2 Corinthians 9:6–7

> "But this I say: He who sows sparingly will also reap sparingly, and he who sows bountifully will also reap bountifully. So let each one give as he purposes in his heart, not grudgingly or of necessity; for God loves a cheerful giver."

Acts 1:8

> "But you shall receive power when the Holy Spirit has come upon you; and you shall be witnesses to Me in Jerusalem, and in all Judea and Samaria, and to the end of the earth."

Philippians 1:21

> "For to me, to live is Christ, and to die is gain."

Matthew 10:32

> "Therefore whoever confesses Me before men, him I will also confess before My Father who is in heaven."

Matthew 25:29

> "For to everyone who has, more will be given, and he will have abundance; but from him who does not have, even what he has will be taken away."

John 14:12

> "Most assuredly, I say to you, he who believes in Me, the works that I do he will do also; and greater works than these he will do, because I go to My Father."

Sticks to the Task

The greatest spiritual truth that I learned from my father is this, "The world is run by those who show up."

Philippians 1:6

> "Being confident of this very thing, that He who has begun a good work in you will complete it until the day of Jesus Christ."

Matthew 5:13–18

> "You are the salt of the earth; but if the salt loses its flavor, how shall it be seasoned? It is then good for nothing but to be thrown out and trampled underfoot by men. "You are the light of the world. A city that is set on a hill cannot be hidden. "Nor do they light a lamp and put it under a basket, but on a lampstand, and it gives light to all who are in the house. "Let your light so shine before men, that they may see your good works and glorify your Father in heaven. "Do not think that I came to destroy the Law or the Prophets. I did not come to

destroy but to fulfill. "For assuredly, I say to you, till heaven and earth pass away, one jot or one tittle will by no means pass from the law till all is fulfilled."

Matthew 7:12–27

"Therefore, whatever you want men to do to you, do also to them, for this is the Law and the Prophets. "Enter by the narrow gate; for wide is the gate and broad is the way that leads to destruction, and there are many who go in by it. "Because narrow is the gate and difficult is the way which leads to life, and there are few who find it. "Beware of false prophets, who come to you in sheep's clothing, but inwardly they are ravenous wolves. "You will know them by their fruits. Do men gather grapes from thornbushes or figs from thistles? "Even so, every good tree bears good fruit, but a bad tree bears bad fruit. "A good tree cannot bear bad fruit, nor can a bad tree bear good fruit. "Every tree that does not bear good fruit is cut down and thrown into the fire. "Therefore by their fruits you will know them. "Not everyone who says to Me, 'Lord, Lord,' shall enter the kingdom of heaven, but he who does the will of My Father in heaven. "Many will say to Me in that day, 'Lord, Lord, have we not prophesied in Your name, cast out demons in Your name, and done many wonders in Your name?' "And then I will declare to them, 'I never knew you; depart from Me, you who practice lawlessness!' "Therefore whoever hears these sayings of Mine, and does them, I will liken him to a wise man who built his house on the rock: "and the rain descended, the floods came, and the winds blew and beat on that house; and it did not fall, for it was founded on the rock. "But everyone who hears these sayings of Mine, and does not do them, will be like a foolish man who built his house on the sand: "and the rain descended, the floods came, and the winds blew and beat on that house; and it fell. And great was its fall."

Mark 12:28–34

"Then one of the scribes came, and having heard them
reasoning together, perceiving that He had answered them
well, asked Him, "Which is the first commandment of all?"
Jesus answered him, "The first of all the commandments is:
'Hear, O Israel, the LORD our God, the LORD is one. 'And
you shall love the LORD your God with all your heart, with
all your soul, with all your mind, and with all your strength.'
This is the first commandment. "And the second, like it, is
this: 'You shall love your neighbor as yourself.' There is no
other commandment greater than these." So the scribe said to
Him, "Well said, Teacher. You have spoken the truth, for
there is one God, and there is no other but He. "And to love
Him with all the heart, with all the understanding, with all the
soul, and with all the strength, and to love one's neighbor as
oneself, is more than all the whole burnt offerings and
sacrifices." Now when Jesus saw that he answered wisely, He
said to him, "You are not far from the kingdom of God." But
after that no one dared question Him."

Romans 13:9–11

"For the commandments, "You shall not commit adultery,"
"You shall not murder," "You shall not steal," "You shall not
bear false witness," "You shall not covet," and if there is any
other commandment, are all summed up in this saying,
namely, "You shall love your neighbor as yourself." Love
does no harm to a neighbor; therefore love is the fulfillment of
the law. And do this, knowing the time, that now it is high
time to awake out of sleep; for now our salvation is nearer
than when we first believed."

1 John 3:3–11

"And everyone who has this hope in Him purifies himself, just
as He is pure. Whoever commits sin also commits lawlessness,
and sin is lawlessness. And you know that He was manifested
to take away our sins, and in Him there is no sin. Whoever
abides in Him does not sin. Whoever sins has neither seen

Him nor known Him. Little children, let no one deceive you. He who practices righteousness is righteous, just as He is righteous. He who sins is of the devil, for the devil has sinned from the beginning. For this purpose the Son of God was manifested, that He might destroy the works of the devil. Whoever has been born of God does not sin, for His seed remains in him; and he cannot sin, because he has been born of God. In this the children of God and the children of the devil are manifest: Whoever does not practice righteousness is not of God, nor is he who does not love his brother. For this is the message that you heard from the beginning, that we should love one another."

Quotes

"Dear Jesus, I thank you that we must come with empty hands. I thank you that you have done all, all on the cross, and that all we need in life or death is to be sure of this."

— Corrie ten Boom

"God hates the lukewarm gospel of half-truths that is now spreading over the globe. This gospel says, 'just believe in Jesus and you'll be saved. There's nothing more to it.' It ignores the whole counsel of God, which speaks of repenting from former sins, of taking up your cross, of being conformed to the image of Christ by the refining work of the Holy Spirit. It is totally silent about the reality of hell and an after-death judgment."

— David Wilkerson

"In conversion you are not attached primarily to an order, nor to an institution, nor a movement, nor a set of beliefs, nor a code of action—you are attached primarily to a person, and secondarily to these other things."

— E. Stanley Jones

"How wonderful to know that when Jesus Christ speaks to you and to me, he enables you to understand yourself, to die to that self because of the cross, and brings the real you to birth."

— Ravi Zacharias

"Divine grace produces holiness of heart and conduct, man is unable to receive without Christ."

— Holy Hubert Lindsey

"The gospel does not save whom it does not sanctify."

— Charles G. Finney

"Ye must be born again."

— George Whitfield

"God shall have all there is of William Booth."

— William Booth

"Salvation comes through a cross and a crucified Christ."

— Andrew Murray

Maxims

- Christ in you is the only hope of *their* glory.
- The name Jesus means, *God saves*.
- We were saved, we are being saved, and we will be saved.
- Salvation is God's provision, coupled with man's responsibility.
- Baptism is as outward expression of inward faith and repentance.
- Baptism is both a wedding and a funeral.

Discussion Questions

1) What are you saved from? What are you saved to?
2) Does man have a part in his salvation, what does God require from us?
3) How does water baptism signify the death, burial, and resurrection of Jesus?

Practical Challenges

1) Ask the Holy Ghost to reveal to you if you are born again. (There's no perhaps, maybe, or I think so): *"The Spirit Himself bears witness with our spirit that we are children of God,"* Romans 8:16.)
2) See, hate, and forsake all known sin. (Repentance means to change your life; it's God's power to stop.)
3) Be baptized publically in water as a testimony and expression of your faith and repentance.
4) Pray earnestly to receive the baptism of the Holy Ghost (with the corresponding evidence). Although one can be saved apart from this baptism, it is not the ideal "normal" salvation God has provided. He want us to be fully empowered for his service and to be His witnesses. The Baptism in the Holy Spirit was common and expected when the book of Acts was written, may it be so with us.

Further Study

Youth Aflame ("Judas" chapter), Winkie Pratney
The Philosophy of the Plan of Salvation, J.B. Walker
So Great Salvation, Charles G. Finney
Bible Doctrines, P.C. Nelson
What Meaneth This?, Carl Brumback
The Essentials of Salvation, Gordon C. Olsen
The Way of Salvation, Albert Barnes
God Has a Right over Our Lives: Lordship, Eli Gautreaux
The Mind of St. Paul ("In Christ" chapter), William Barclay
In Christ, E. Stanley Jones
Conversion, E. Stanley Jones
The Normal Christian Birth (Book and YouTube Series), David Pawson
Sharing Your Faith (Conference lecture on YouTube), Gordon C. Olson
The God They Never Knew, George Otis, Jr.
The Marks of the New Birth, John Wesley
21st Century Reformation (PDF), Winkie Pratney

CHAPTER 7: LORDSHIP
Section 2: Our Response

Words like "lord," "master," and "king" have little to no meaning in our western context, yet the scriptures are full of these descriptors for Jesus of Nazareth. America is swamped with the idea and message that Jesus is a Savior. It's proclaimed from every steeple, seminary, and pulpit, and yet the great necessary and complementary truth of his lordship is thundered by a few—by a remnant. May we come to learn that he is both Lord and Savior and be reminded of the great truth that if he's not your Lord, he cannot be your Savior. You can't invite him to be one and not the other; they are one and the same. The Lord said these sober and powerful words:

"But why do you call Me 'Lord, Lord,' and not do the things which I say?"

— Jesus, Luke 6:46

Scriptures

Philippians 2:10

"That at the name of Jesus every knee should bow, of those in heaven, and of those on earth, and of those under the earth."

Acts 9:6

"So he, trembling and astonished, said, "Lord, what do You want me to do?" Then the Lord said to him, "Arise and go into the city, and you will be told what you must do.""

Romans 14:8–9

"For if we live, we live to the Lord; and if we die, we die to the Lord. Therefore, whether we live or die, we are the Lord's. For to this end Christ died and rose and lived again, that He might be Lord of both the dead and the living."

Acts 2:36

> "Therefore let all the house of Israel know assuredly that God has made this Jesus, whom you crucified, both Lord and Christ."

Luke 6:46

> "But why do you call Me 'Lord, Lord,' and not do the things which I say?"

Hebrews 5:9

> "And having been perfected, He became the author of eternal salvation to all who obey Him."

1 Corinthians 7:22–23

> "For he who is called in the Lord while a slave is the Lord's freedman. Likewise he who is called while free is Christ's slave. You were bought at a price; do not become slaves of men."

Revelation 19:6

> "And I heard, as it were, the voice of a great multitude, as the sound of many waters and as the sound of mighty thunderings, saying, "Alleluia! For the Lord God Omnipotent reigns!"

Deuteronomy 10:12

> "And now, Israel, what does the LORD your God require of you, but to fear the LORD your God, to walk in all His ways and to love Him, to serve the LORD your God with all your heart and with all your soul."

1 John 2:15

> "Do not love the world or the things in the world. If anyone loves the world, the love of the Father is not in him."

Quotes

"Unless Jesus is Lord of all, he is not Lord at all."

— S.M. Zwemer

"The greatness of a man's power is the measure of his surrender." — William Booth

"It is either all of Christ or none of Christ! I believe we need to preach again a whole Christ to the world—a Christ who does not need our apologies, a Christ who will not be divided, a Christ who will either be Lord of all or will not be Lord at all!"

— A.W. Tozer

"A crucified man loses all his rights."

— Leonard Ravenhill

"Anything you love more than Jesus Christ is an idol."

— Leonard Ravenhill

"God's right is founded in his value."

— Winkie Pratney

"The lordship of Jesus Christ is not quite forgotten among Christians, but it has been relegated to the hymnal where all responsibility toward it may be comfortably discharged in a glow of religious emotion. Or if it is taught as a theory in the classroom it is rarely applied to practical living. The idea that the man Christ Jesus has absolute final authority over the whole church and over its members in every detail of their lives is simply not now accepted as true by the rank and file of evangelical Christians."

— A.W. Tozer

"Until the will and the affections are brought under the authority of Christ, we have not begun to understand, let alone to accept, his lordship."

— Elisabeth Elliot

"When Jesus is truly our lord, he directs our lives and we gladly obey him. Indeed, we bring every part of our lives under his lordship—our home and family, our sexuality and marriage, our job or unemployment, our money and possessions, our ambitions and recreations."

— John R.W. Stott

"That's what lordship is—Christ reigning as supreme authority over our life. Making Jesus lord of our life is not something passive. It's not a state of being; it's a state of doing. Those whom Jesus recognizes as his own are those who do the will of his Father in heaven."

— Keith Green

"Only the believing obey, only the obedient believe."

— Dietrich Bonhoeffer

Maxims

- There is a link between salvation and lordship—you can't have one without the other.
- Obedience comes before knowledge.
- Everyone wants a savior; no one wants a Lord.
- Jesus is Lord: We don't make him Lord or accept him as Lord; he is the Lord.
- "Jesus is Lord" is and will always be the battle cry of the blood-bought church of God.

Discussion Questions

1) Is there anything in your life that competes with Christ for your allegiance?
2) Why do you do the things you do? And who do you do them for?
3) What right does Jesus have to rule your life?

Practical Challenges

1) Share your newfound salvation through Christ with seven separate people. The purpose of your testimony is to share it. If you are not a new believer still complete this challenge to rekindle the flame of your first love. Remember in the Kingdom you only have what you share.
2) Ask a spiritual mentor to honestly comment on a weakness that he sees in your walk.
3) Ask yourself, "Am I serving Christ sacrificially, or comfortably?" (Make a change/tell your mentor.)

Further Study

So Great Salvation, Charles G. Finney
The God They Never Knew, George Otis, Jr.
Youth Aflame, Winkie Pratney
True and False Conversion, Charles G. Finney
Free as a Slave (Ministry tract), Winkie Pratney
No Compromise, Keith Green
The Greatest Faith Ever Known, Fulton Oursler
The Mind of St. Paul, William Barclay
The Normal Christian Birth, David Pawson
Sharing your Faith (Conference lecture on YouTube*)*, Gordon C. Olson
The Cost of Discipleship, Dietrich Bonhoeffer
God Has a Right over Our Lives: Lordship, Eli Gautreaux
The Truth Shall Make You Free, Gordon C. Olson
21st Century Reformation (PDF), Winkie Pratney

CHAPTER 8: THE BAPTISM IN THE HOLY SPIRIT

Prior to Jesus' ascension, Christ commanded his disciples to wait in Jerusalem for "power from on high." This baptism of power transforms believers, and equips them for their mission of service and proclamation. Supernatural evidence has always followed this dynamic event, which transforms individuals, households, and nations. The evidence of this baptism takes the most unruly of man's members, "the untamable tongue," and brings it under the Spirit's submission and authority. The symbol of rebellion is redeemed into a fountain of intimacy and power. You, who are seeking to enter into the fullness, must trust the promises of God: that he will baptize you with the Holy Spirit and with fire.

Scriptures

The Baptism in the Holy Spirit

This precious gift of the Father, came into the early church on the day of Pentecost. Clarity is needed in distinguishing between the Holy Spirit's role in salvation – with marking believers with the seal of ownership – and the eminent empowerment through the Spirit's baptism. Although the baptism of the Holy Spirit is a separate and distinct work apart from salvation, it should be a part of the normal Christian birth experience.

Matthew 3:11

> "I indeed baptize you with water unto repentance, but He who is coming after me is mightier than I, whose sandals I am not worthy to carry. He will baptize you with the Holy Spirit and fire."

Mark 1:8

> "I indeed baptized you with water, but He will baptize you with the Holy Spirit."

Luke 24:49

"Behold, I send the Promise of My Father upon you; but tarry in the city of Jerusalem until you are endued with power from on high."

John 14:19–21, 26

"A little while longer and the world will see Me no more, but you will see Me. Because I live, you will live also. "At that day you will know that I am in My Father, and you in Me, and I in you. "He who has My commandments and keeps them, it is he who loves Me. And he who loves Me will be loved by My Father, and I will love him and manifest Myself to him." ... "But the Helper, the Holy Spirit, whom the Father will send in My name, He will teach you all things, and bring to your remembrance all things that I said to you."

John 16:13

" However, when He, the Spirit of truth, has come, He will guide you into all truth; for He will not speak on His own *authority,* but whatever He hears He will speak; and He will tell you things to come."

Acts 1:4–5

"And being assembled together with them, He commanded them not to depart from Jerusalem, but to wait for the Promise of the Father, "which," He said, "you have heard from Me; "for John truly baptized with water, but you shall be baptized with the Holy Spirit not many days from now."

Acts 1:8

"But you shall receive power when the Holy Spirit has come upon you; and you shall be witnesses to Me in Jerusalem, and in all Judea and Samaria, and to the end of the earth."

Acts 2:1–12

"When the Day of Pentecost had fully come, they were all with one accord in one place. And suddenly there came a sound from heaven, as of a rushing mighty wind, and it filled the whole house where they were sitting. Then there appeared to them divided tongues, as of fire, and one sat upon each of them. And they were all filled with the Holy Spirit and began to speak with other tongues, as the Spirit gave them utterance. And there were dwelling in Jerusalem Jews, devout men, from every nation under heaven. And when this sound occurred, the multitude came together, and were confused, because everyone heard them speak in his own language. Then they were all amazed and marveled, saying to one another, "Look, are not all these who speak Galileans? "And how is it that we hear, each in our own language in which we were born? "Parthians and Medes and Elamites, those dwelling in Mesopotamia, Judea and Cappadocia, Pontus and Asia, "Phrygia and Pamphylia, Egypt and the parts of Libya adjoining Cyrene, visitors from Rome, both Jews and proselytes, "Cretans and Arabs--we hear them speaking in our own tongues the wonderful works of God." So they were all amazed and perplexed, saying to one another, "Whatever could this mean?"

Acts 2:38–39

"Then Peter said to them, "Repent, and let every one of you be baptized in the name of Jesus Christ for the remission of sins; and you shall receive the gift of the Holy Spirit. "For the promise is to you and to your children, and to all who are afar off, as many as the Lord our God will call."

The Evidence

The overwhelming corresponding evidence recorded in the history of the apostles, is that supernatural empowered speech proceeds from the baptism in the Holy Spirit. The initial evidence throughout the Acts narrative and church history is that the believers are empowered to speak in tongues. This gift from the Father opens up a fountain of living water, where intimacy flourishes through prayer in the Spirit. Although tongues remains biblically the initial evidence of the Spirit's baptism, the corresponding evidence of prophecy, proclamation and boldness must not be sidelined and neglected. We must maintain an attitude of humility and gratefulness in all matters regarding the Spirit. There is no place for division or superiority, we are all "learners."

Acts 8:17–19

"Then they laid hands on them, and they received the Holy Spirit. And when Simon saw that through the laying on of the apostles' hands the Holy Spirit was given, he offered them money, saying, "Give me this power also, that anyone on whom I lay hands may receive the Holy Spirit."

Acts 10:44–46

"While Peter was still speaking these words, the Holy Spirit fell upon all those who heard the word. And those of the circumcision who believed were astonished, as many as came with Peter, because the gift of the Holy Spirit had been poured out on the Gentiles also. For they heard them speak with tongues and magnify God. Then Peter answered."

Acts 19:1–6

"And it happened, while Apollos was at Corinth, that Paul, having passed through the upper regions, came to Ephesus. And finding some disciples he said to them, "Did you receive the Holy Spirit when you believed?" So they said to him, "We have not so much as heard whether there is a Holy Spirit." And he said to them, "Into what then were you baptized?" So they said, "Into John's baptism." Then Paul said, "John indeed baptized with a baptism of repentance, saying to the people that they should believe on Him who would come after him, that is, on Christ Jesus." When they heard this, they were baptized in the name of the Lord Jesus. And when Paul had laid hands on them, the Holy Spirit came upon them, and they spoke with tongues and prophesied."

John 7:37–39

> "On the last day, that great day of the feast, Jesus stood and cried out, saying, "If anyone thirsts, let him come to Me and drink. "He who believes in Me, as the Scripture has said, out of his heart will flow rivers of living water." But this He spoke concerning the Spirit, whom those believing in Him would receive; for the Holy Spirit was not yet given, because Jesus was not yet glorified."

Acts 2:4

> "And they were all filled with the Holy Spirit and began to speak with other tongues, as the Spirit gave them utterance."

1 Corinthians 14:18

> "I thank my God I speak with tongues more than you all."

Mark 16:17–18

> "And these signs will follow those who believe: In My name they will cast out demons; they will speak with new tongues; "they will take up serpents; and if they drink anything deadly, it will by no means hurt them; they will lay hands on the sick, and they will recover."

Insights into Receiving the Baptism in the Holy Spirit

Faith

We must have the confidence that God means what he says. We must trust in His word that this promise of the Spirit, as it was poured out on the day of Pentecost, will continue to pour out into hearts filled with faith and adoration. The word of God says in the Book of Acts, "For the promise is to you and to your children, and to all who are afar off, as many as the Lord our God will call."

Luke 11:9–13

> "So I say to you, ask, and it will be given to you; seek, and you will find; knock, and it will be opened to you. "For everyone who asks receives, and he who seeks finds, and to

him who knocks it will be opened. "If a son asks for bread from any father among you, will he give him a stone? Or if he asks for a fish, will he give him a serpent instead of a fish? "Or if he asks for an egg, will he offer him a scorpion? "If you then, being evil, know how to give good gifts to your children, how much more will your heavenly Father give the Holy Spirit to those who ask Him!"

Acts 1:8

"But you shall receive power when the Holy Spirit has come upon you; and you shall be witnesses to Me in Jerusalem, and in all Judea and Samaria, and to the end of the earth."

Gratitude

In my years of ministry I cannot begin to count the men and women who have been filled and baptized with the fullness of God's Spirit through the conviction of gratitude. We must get our eyes off ourselves and unto Jesus, and focus on the love we have for each other. It's in this grateful heart of humility and love that the Spirit erupts into a joyful adoration for Jesus and what he has done.

2 Corinthians 9:15

"Thanks be to God for His indescribable gift!"

James 1:17

"Every good gift and every perfect gift is from above, and comes down from the Father of lights, with whom there is no variation or shadow of turning."

Psalm 100:4–5

"Enter into His gates with thanksgiving, And into His courts with praise. Be thankful to Him, and bless His name. For the LORD is good; His mercy is everlasting, And His truth endures to all generations."

Obedience

Roadblocks and hindrances to the baptism of the Holy Spirit can be unforgiveness or unconfessed sin. It was only when the disciples were waiting in Jerusalem, being obedient to the command of Christ, that they receive the blessing of Pentecost.

Acts 5:32

> "And we are His witnesses to these things, and so also is the Holy Spirit whom God has given to those who obey Him."

John 7:39

> "But this He spoke concerning the Spirit, whom those believing in Him would receive; for the Holy Spirit was not yet given, because Jesus was not yet glorified."

Joel 2:28

> "And it shall come to pass afterward That I will pour out My Spirit on all flesh; Your sons and your daughters shall prophesy, Your old men shall dream dreams, Your young men shall see visions."

Participation

God desires that we ask Jesus, the Baptizer, to fill us with the Holy Spirit. Sometimes people wait in silence for God to take over their voice. However, God waits for our willing and joyful participation with the Holy Spirit in praying with other tongues. It's the principle of participation that is woven into the Spirit filled life.

Quotes

"The only evidence of the Holy Spirit in your life is a holy life."
— Leonard Ravenhill

"When you strip it of everything else, Pentecost stands for power and life. That's what came into the church when the Holy Spirit came down on the day of Pentecost."

— David Wilkerson

"The baptism of the Holy Spirit is more of the same God you already know."

— Ryan Volkmer

"The Holy Spirit is the gift of the risen Christ. His anointing, filling and empowering work, acts as a baptism of love that gives power to make Jesus real to you and known to others."

— Winkie Pratney

"Just as the Lord Jesus gave the Holy Spirit to Peter, he is willing to give the Holy Spirit to you. Are you willing to receive him? Are you willing to give up yourself entirely as an empty, helpless vessel, to receive the power of the Holy Spirit, to live, to dwell, and to work in you every day? Dear believer, God has prepared such a beautiful and such a blessed life for every one of us, and God as a Father is waiting to see why you will not come to him and let him fill you with the Holy Ghost."

— Andrew Murray

"Take a piece of charcoal, and however much you may wash it its blackness will not disappear, but let the fire enter into it and its dark colour vanishes. So also when the sinner receives the Holy Spirit (who is from the Father and Myself, for the Father and I are one), which is the baptism of fire, all the blackness of sin is driven away, and he is made a light to the world, As the fire in the charcoal, so I abide in My children and they in Me, and through them I make Myself manifest to the world."

— Sadhu Sundar Singh

"Before we go to our knees to receive the baptism of fire, let me beg of you to see to it that your souls are in harmony with the will and purpose of the Holy Spirit whom you seek."

— William Booth

"The baptism with the Holy Spirit is always connected with, and is primarily for the purpose of, equipment for testimony and service: it is to make us useful for God in the salvation of souls and not merely to make us happy."

— R.A. Torrey

"A church in the land without the Spirit is rather a curse than a blessing. If you have not the Spirit of God, Christian worker, remember that you stand in somebody else's way; you are a fruitless tree standing where a fruitful tree might grow."

— C.H. Spurgeon

"The very fact that we believe one thing and some of us another does not do away with the fact that GOD says -" Be filled with the Spirit". I believe that is the greatest need of the church of Jesus Christ today. Everywhere I go, I find God's people lack something: God's people are hungry for something. Many of us say that our Christian experience is not all that we expected. We have oft-recurring defeat in our lives, and as a result across the country from coast to coast there are hundreds of Christian people hungry for something we do not have. ...I am persuaded that our desperate need tonight is not a new organization, a new movement - or even a new method. We have enough of these. I believe the greatest need tonight is that men and women who profess the Name of Jesus Christ be filled with the Spirit! We are trying to do the work of God without supernatural power. It cannot be done! When God told us to go and preach the Gospel to "every creature: and to evangelize the world, He provided supernatural power for us. That power is given to us by the Holy Spirit. It is more powerful than atomic power...It is more potent than any explosive made by man. Do you know anything of the power of the Holy Spirit?"

— Billy Graham

Maxims

- Seek the giver, not the gift.

- He will baptize you; He's not just thinking about it.
- God always interprets you rightly.
- You will know that you know that you know; "dynamite."
- Power to witness, power to serve.
- Tongues are personal, partnership, and powerful.

Discussion Questions

1) Is the baptism in the Holy Spirit for all believers today? Where does it say that in scripture?
2) Why does God use the tongue as one of the evidences of the baptism in the Holy Spirit?
3) Do you have power to witness that has come from this baptism of love and power?
4) What does it mean to pray in the Spirit (Jude 20, 1 Cor 14:14)?

Practical Challenges

1) Pray for at least one hour to receive the baptism of the Holy Spirit.
2) Have those who are filled with the Holy Spirit lay hands on you in prayer.
3) Express gratitude in prayer to those who minister to you.
4) Sing songs of gratitude in praise to Jesus. Sing the words the Spirit impresses on your heart. (Eph 5:18-20).
5) Pray in faith. (Gal 3:14).

Further Study

Power for Life, Jeff Leake
What Meaneth This?, Carl Brumback
They Speak with Other Tongues, John L. Sherrill
Bible Doctrines (Chapter 8: "The Baptism of the Holy Spirit"), P.C. Nelson
Bible Doctrines (Chapter : 7 "The Promise of the Father"), P.C. Nelson
Living in the Spirit, George O. Wood
The Normal Christian Birth, David Pawson
Pentecost, Leonard Ravenhill
Power from God, Winkie Pratney

Chapter 8: The Baptism in the Holy Spirit

The Holy Spirit, R.A. Torrey
The Way to Pentecost, Samuel Chadwick
Surprised by the Power of the Spirit, Jack Deere
How to be Filled with the Holy Spirit, A.W. Tozer
Speaking in Tongues, Larry Christenson
The Spirit Himself, R.M. Riggs
Knowing the Doctrines of the Bible, Myer Pearlman
Systematic Theology (Vol 3), Ernest S. Williams
Aglow with the Spirit, Dr. Robert Frost
The Master Plan of Discipleship, (Chapter 6), Robert E. Coleman
The Baptism with the Holy Spirit, R.A. Torrey
The Spirit of Christ, Andrew Murray
Bible Readings on Holiness, Basil Miller
Deeper Experiences of Famous Christians, James G. Lawson
Spiritual Leadership (Chapter 10), Oswald J. Sanders
Acts Commentary, Stanley M. Horton
Our Distinctive Doctrine: The Baptism in the Holy Spirit, Assemblies of
    God

CHAPTER 9: THE BIBLE

The scriptures have an unsurpassable place in literature of the world. No other book in the history of mankind has sold more copies and transformed more characters than the Holy Bible. It is smuggled, stolen, and outlawed. It revolutionizes nations, governments and kingdoms. It established our legal system, and inspired our literary poets and artistic masters. It is a collective masterpiece in its own right, spanning two thousand years in its compilation. It covers the entire scope of human existence from creation to final judgment. In its infinite wisdom it sufficiently answers the deepest philosophical questions of man: from meaning, morality, origin and destiny. It is the book of books, it's the word of the living God.

Scriptures

2 Timothy 3:16

"All Scripture is given by inspiration of God, and is profitable for doctrine, for reproof, for correction, for instruction in righteousness."

2 Timothy 2:15

"Be diligent to present yourself approved to God, a worker who does not need to be ashamed, rightly dividing the word of truth."

Hebrews 4:12–13

"For the word of God is living and powerful, and sharper than any two-edged sword, piercing even to the division of soul and spirit, and of joints and marrow, and is a discerner of the thoughts and intents of the heart. And there is no creature hidden from His sight, but all things are naked and open to the eyes of Him to whom we must give account."

Psalm 119:11

"Your word I have hidden in my heart, That I might not sin against You."

John 10:35

"If He called them gods, to whom the word of God came (and the Scripture cannot be broken)."

2 Peter 1:20–21

"Knowing this first, that no prophecy of Scripture is of any private interpretation, for prophecy never came by the will of man, but holy men of God spoke as they were moved by the Holy Spirit."

John 5:39

"You search the Scriptures, for in them you think you have eternal life; and these are they which testify of Me."

Psalm 119:105

"Your word is a lamp to my feet And a light to my path."

John 20:31

"But these are written that you may believe that Jesus is the Christ, the Son of God, and that believing you may have life in His name."

Matthew 24:35

"Heaven and earth will pass away, but My words will by no means pass away."

Isaiah 40:8

"The grass withers, the flower fades, But the word of our God stands forever."

1 Peter 1:25

"But the word of the LORD endures forever." Now this is the word which by the gospel was preached to you."

John 6:63

"It is the Spirit who gives life; the flesh profits nothing. The words that I speak to you are spirit, and they are life."

Quotes

"The Bible contains the mind of God, the state of man, the way of salvation, the doom of sinners, and the happiness of believers. Its doctrines are holy, its precepts are binding, its histories are true, and its decisions are immutable. Read it to be wise, believe it to be safe, and practice it to be holy. It contains light to direct you, food to support you, and comfort to cheer you. It is the traveler's map, the pilgrim's staff, the pilot's compass, the soldier's sword, and the Christian's charter. Here paradise is restored, heaven opened, and the gates of hell disclosed. Christ is its grand subject, our good the design, and the glory of God its end. It should fill the memory, rule the heart, and guide the feet. Read it slowly, frequently and prayerfully. It is a mine of wealth, a paradise of glory and a river of pleasure. It is given you in life, will be opened at the judgment, and be remembered forever. It involves the highest responsibility, will reward the greatest labor, and will contend all who trifle with its sacred contents."

— The Gideons

"One of these days some simple soul will pick up the book of God, read it, and believe it. Then the rest of us will be embarrassed."

— Leonard Ravenhill

"66 books by 40 authors and we now find that it (the Bible) is an integrated message system from outside our time domain."

— Chuck Missler

"The word of God well understood and religiously obeyed is the shortest route to spiritual perfection. And we must not select a few favorite passages to the exclusion of others. Nothing less than a whole Bible can make a whole Christian."

— A.W. Tozer

"Let me be a man of one book."

— John Wesley

"It's not a book of history; although, its records have been accurately substantiated by modern archaeology. It is not a book of poetry; although, it has been the inspiration of countless songs and poems through the centuries. It is not an adventure story; although, few novels have matched the sheer drama of its pages. It is not a book of ethics or morality; although, civilization's finest and fairest laws have been forged from its principles. It is not a textbook, but it still astonishes scientists and scholars from fields as widely-differing as genetics, geology and nuclear physics. The Bible is a unique record of man's problem and God's own answer; the Good News of salvation from sin through Jesus."

— Winkie Pratney

"The Bible is not an end in itself, but a means to bring men to an intimate and satisfying knowledge of God, that they may enter into him, that they may delight in his presence, may taste and know the inner sweetness of the very God himself in the core and center of their hearts."

— A.W. Tozer

"The Bible is the written word of God, and because it is written it is confined and limited by the necessities of ink and paper and leather. The voice of God, however, is alive and free as the sovereign God is free. '*The words that I speak unto you, they are spirit, and they are life.*' The life is in the speaking words. God's word in the Bible can have power only because it corresponds to God's word in the universe. It is the present voice, which makes the written word powerful. Otherwise it would lay locked in slumber within the covers of a book."

— A.W. Tozer

"The whole meaning of spiritual understanding is that we see what the Spirit has always meant. It is one of our laws of interpretation that the whole Bible is focused in Christ, and that the work of the Holy Spirit in every dispensation relates to Christ."

— T. Austin-Sparks

"Doctrinal rightness and rightness of ecclesiastical position are important, but only as a starting point to go on into a living relationship—and not as ends in themselves."

— Francis Schaeffer

"It is the Most Beautiful Story ever told. It is the Best Guide to human conduct ever known. It gives a Meaning, and a Glow, and a Joy, and a Victory, and a Destiny, and a Glory, to Life elsewhere unknown."

— H.H. Halley

"The inspiration of the Bible is proved by experience, not by logic. 'Meditate therein day and night' to obey, to do according to all that is 'written therein,' and you shall know, you shall taste its sweetness, behold its wonders, and hear in its words the whisperings of the everlasting Father to the heart of his child."

— Samuel Logan Brengle

"Does the Bible offer hope to the sinner? The man who has wasted his life, scorned the voice of conscience, turned his back on light and goodness and God? It is the only book in the world that does. It, and it alone, tells of a redeeming God, a Saviour from sin, a loving heavenly Father who waits to welcome sinners."

— Samuel Logan Brengle

"We must affirm the inerrancy of Scripture and then live under it."

— Francis Schaeffer

"The Bible is to me the most precious thing in the world just because it tells me the story of Jesus."

— George MacDonald

"Man shall not live by bread alone,' said Jesus, 'but by every word that proceedeth out of the mouth of God.' Does the Bible feed the soul of man? All the saints and soldiers of Jesus of all the ages

have been nourished and have lived on the word of God."

— Samuel Logan Brengle

Maxims

- The Bible is either absolute or obsolete.
- All truth is God's truth.
- The best way to read the Bible is obediently.
- The Bible isn't a book; it's a library.
- The best commentary for the Bible is the Bible itself.
- The Old Testament is in the New Testament revealed, and the New Testament is the Old Testament concealed.
- The Bible is the inspired, inerrant, infallible word of God.

Discussion Questions

1) How would you respond if you were challenged with the objection that the Bible has been changed throughout the centuries?
2) Can we, as a small group, go through the entire Bible, book by book, and create an overview mapping out God's plan of redemption?
3) Why do you believe the Bible is the inspired word of God?

Practical Challenges

1) Develop a color-coded theme system for highlighting scripture.
2) Develop a systematic reading plan. (Five chapters a day gets you through in a year.)
3) Carry your Bible with you everywhere for a week. (No backpack, bag, or briefcase)
4) Teach the S.O.A.P. method to a young believer. (Write the **scripture** down, Record your **observation**, discover the personal **application** to your life, and dedicate what you learned in **prayer** to God.)

Further Study

Youth Aflame ("Thomas" chapter), Winkie Pratney
Nave's Topical Bible, Orville J. Nave
Thebibleproject.com

Blueletterbible.org
Biblehub.com
Understanding the Bible, John R.W. Stott
Spiritual Leadership (Chapter 13), Oswald J. Sanders
What the Bible Teaches, R.A. Torrey
The Daily Study Bible Series, William Barclay
Learn the Bible in 24 Hours, Chuck Missler
The New Evidence that Demands a Verdict, Josh McDowell
The Battle for the Bible, Harold Lindsell
New Testament History, F.F. Bruce
The Books and the Parchments, F.F. Bruce
How We Got Our Bible (PDF), Chuck Missler
Wholly Bible, Holy True (Article), Winkie Pratney
Unlocking the Bible, David Pawson
Halley's Bible Handbook, H.H. Halley
All the Doctrines of the Bible, Herbert Lockyer
The Testimony of the Organic Unity of the Bible to its Inspiration, A.T.
    Pierson
The Pulpit Commentary, Compiled by Rev. Joseph S. Exell and Henry
    Donald Maurice
The New Testament Documents: Are They Reliable?, F.F. Bruce
*The Complete Works of Francis Schaeffer: Vol 2: A Christian View of the
    Bible as Truth*

CHAPTER 10: THE CHURCH

The Church is God's agency of reconciliation. It is made up of called-out ones, purchased by the blood of the Lamb. They are set apart to the special work of advancing the kingdom of God. These believers constitute the body of Christ on the earth; each unique member has a significant role in the body for the act of reconciliation. By pledging allegiance to the head of the body, Christ Jesus, one is incorporated into the spiritual family of God. Remembering Paul's admonition, *"Endeavoring to keep the unity of the Spirit in the bond of peace,"* this corporate body unified in purpose and adoration ultimately will express the fullness of the kingdom of God on earth.

Scriptures

God's Agency of Reconciliation

Ephesians 2:18–22

> "For through Him we both have access by one Spirit to the Father. Now, therefore, you are no longer strangers and foreigners, but fellow citizens with the saints and members of the household of God, having been built on the foundation of the apostles and prophets, Jesus Christ Himself being the chief cornerstone, in whom the whole building, being fitted together, grows into a holy temple in the Lord, in whom you also are being built together for a dwelling place of God in the Spirit."

Hebrews 10:25

> "Not forsaking the assembling of ourselves together, as is the manner of some, but exhorting one another, and so much the more as you see the Day approaching."

Ephesians 4:1–16

> "I, therefore, the prisoner of the Lord, beseech you to walk worthy of the calling with which you were called, with all lowliness and gentleness, with longsuffering, bearing with one

another in love, endeavoring to keep the unity of the Spirit in the bond of peace. There is one body and one Spirit, just as you were called in one hope of your calling; one Lord, one faith, one baptism; one God and Father of all, who is above all, and through all, and in you all. But to each one of us grace was given according to the measure of Christ's gift. Therefore He says: "When He ascended on high, He led captivity captive, And gave gifts to men." (Now this, "He ascended"-- what does it mean but that He also first descended into the lower parts of the earth? He who descended is also the One who ascended far above all the heavens, that He might fill all things.) And He Himself gave some to be apostles, some prophets, some evangelists, and some pastors and teachers, for the equipping of the saints for the work of ministry, for the edifying of the body of Christ, till we all come to the unity of the faith and of the knowledge of the Son of God, to a perfect man, to the measure of the stature of the fullness of Christ; that we should no longer be children, tossed to and fro and carried about with every wind of doctrine, by the trickery of men, in the cunning craftiness of deceitful plotting, but, speaking the truth in love, may grow up in all things into Him who is the head--Christ-- from whom the whole body, joined and knit together by what every joint supplies, according to the effective working by which every part does its share, causes growth of the body for the edifying of itself in love."

Revelation 19:7–9

"Let us be glad and rejoice and give Him glory, for the marriage of the Lamb has come, and His wife has made herself ready." And to her it was granted to be arrayed in fine linen, clean and bright, for the fine linen is the righteous acts of the saints. Then he said to me, "Write: 'Blessed are those who are called to the marriage supper of the Lamb!' " And he said to me, "These are the true sayings of God."

Revelation 21:9

"Then one of the seven angels who had the seven bowls filled with the seven last plagues came to me and talked with me, saying, "Come, I will show you the bride, the Lamb's wife."

Ephesians 5:25–32

"Husbands, love your wives, just as Christ also loved the church and gave Himself for her, that He might sanctify and cleanse her with the washing of water by the word, that He might present her to Himself a glorious church, not having spot or wrinkle or any such thing, but that she should be holy and without blemish. So husbands ought to love their own wives as their own bodies; he who loves his wife loves himself. For no one ever hated his own flesh, but nourishes and cherishes it, just as the Lord does the church. For we are members of His body, of His flesh and of His bones. "For this reason a man shall leave his father and mother and be joined to his wife, and the two shall become one flesh." This is a great mystery, but I speak concerning Christ and the church."

Ephesians 1:22

"And He put all things under His feet, and gave Him to be head over all things to the church."

1 Corinthians 4:1

"Let a man so consider us, as servants of Christ and stewards of the mysteries of God."

Names for the Redeemed

The Body of Christ

Romans 12:4-5

"For as we have many members in one body, but all the members do not have the same function, so we, being many, are one body in Christ, and individually members of one another."

Colossians 1:18

"And He is the head of the body, the church, who is the

beginning, the firstborn from the dead, that in all things He may have the preeminence."

1 Corinthians 12:12
"For as the body is one and has many members, but all the members of that one body, being many, are one body, so also is Christ."

Household of God

Ephesians 2:19
"Now, therefore, you are no longer strangers and foreigners, but fellow citizens with the saints and members of the household of God."

House of God/Church of the Living God

1 Timothy 3:15
"But if I am delayed, I write so that you may know how you ought to conduct yourself in the house of God, which is the church of the living God, the pillar and ground of the truth."

Hebrews 10:21
"And having a High Priest over the house of God."

Church of God

Acts 20:28
"Therefore take heed to yourselves and to all the flock, among which the Holy Spirit has made you overseers, to shepherd the church of God which He purchased with His own blood."

Church/General Assembly of the Firstborn

Hebrews 12:23
"To the general assembly and church of the firstborn who are

registered in heaven, to God the Judge of all, to the spirits of just men made perfect."

City of the Living God

Hebrews 12:22
> "But you have come to Mount Zion and to the city of the living God, the heavenly Jerusalem, to an innumerable company of angels."

Congregation of Saints

Psalm 149:1
> "Praise the LORD! Sing to the LORD a new song, And His praise in the assembly of saints."

The Flock of God

1 Peter 5:2
> "Shepherd the flock of God which is among you, serving as overseers, not by compulsion but willingly, not for dishonest gain but eagerly."

Lamb's Wife/the Bride

Revelation 19:7
> "Let us be glad and rejoice and give Him glory, for the marriage of the Lamb has come, and His wife has made herself ready."

Revelation 21:9
> "Then one of the seven angels who had the seven bowls filled with the seven last plagues came to me and talked with me, saying, "Come, I will show you the bride, the Lamb's wife."

Temple of God

1 Corinthians 3:16–17
> "Do you not know that you are the temple of God and that the Spirit of God dwells in you? If anyone defiles the temple of God, God will destroy him. For the temple of God is holy, which temple you are."

2 Corinthians 6:16
> "And what agreement has the temple of God with idols? For you are the temple of the living God. As God has said: "I will dwell in them And walk among them. I will be their God, And they shall be My people."

Apostolic Ministry

Ephesians 4:11–16
> "And He Himself gave some to be apostles, some prophets, some evangelists, and some pastors and teachers, for the equipping of the saints for the work of ministry, for the edifying of the body of Christ, till we all come to the unity of the faith and of the knowledge of the Son of God, to a perfect man, to the measure of the stature of the fullness of Christ; that we should no longer be children, tossed to and fro and carried about with every wind of doctrine, by the trickery of men, in the cunning craftiness of deceitful plotting, but, speaking the truth in love, may grow up in all things into Him who is the head--Christ-- from whom the whole body, joined and knit together by what every joint supplies, according to the effective working by which every part does its share, causes growth of the body for the edifying of itself in love."

Good Wisdom in Choosing a Church

Remember, it is not about who is preaching, it is about what is being preached.

These elements compiled by Pastor Mark Driscoll:

Character in leadership: Do they fear God—do they love people?
Clarity of content: Clear, good, content in light of eternity.
Consistency: How long have they been serving their community?
Courage: How are they advancing the kingdom of Christ?
Christ-centered: Is Christ the end and means of the ministry?

Good Wisdom in Serving the Church

Commit for the long haul, no transitory, flippant, or immature service.
Serve the bride of Christ with commitment and faithfulness.
This concept can best be described as marriage. We must marry our
local church. Be fruitful and loyal to this localized expression of the
body of Christ. The greatest fruit comes after the toughest storms.
How you treat your local body is exactly how you treat Christ.

A great analysis of Christian maturity is evaluating yourself,
regarding these three proven measures of **Commitment.**

Are you in Fellowship? Not mere attendance, but rather in deep
meaningful relationships where you are vulnerable regarding your
walk with Jesus.

Are you Generous? Do you honor Jesus through your finances? We
all get the privilege to contribute to the advancement of God's
kingdom. Where your treasure is there your heart is also.

Are you Serving? Following Christ means following him into
service. We get the great privilege to serve God by serving each other.

Quotes

"There are those, particularly in our day, who are so disenchanted
with the visible church that they steadfastly refuse to join any local
church. Such a posture is misguided and involves overt disobedience
to the commands of Christ. Though it is possible for a believer to be
confused about this for a season, someone who persists

in such a posture is, in all probability, not a believer. It is the duty of every Christian to join a visible church."

— J.C. Ryle

"The Bible knows nothing of solitary religion."

— John Wesley

"What the church needs today is not more machinery or better, not new organizations or more and novel methods, but men whom the Holy Ghost can use—men of prayer, men mighty in prayer. The Holy Ghost does not flow through methods, but through men. He does not come on machinery, but on men. He does not anoint plans, but men, men of prayer."

— E.M. Bounds

"The church is the body of Christ, and the Spirit is the Spirit of Christ. He fills the body, directs its movements, controls its members, inspires its wisdom, and supplies its strength. He guides into truth, sanctifies its agents, and empowers for witnessing. The Spirit has never abdicated his authority nor relegated his power."

— Samuel Chadwick

"When a church is truly convinced that prayer is where the action is, that church will so construct its corporate activities that the prayer program will have the highest priority."

— Paul E. Billheimer

"The church is the only society that exists for the benefit of those who are not its members."

— William Temple

"We must cease to think of the church as a gathering of institutions and organizations, and we must get back to the notion that we are the people of God."

— Martyn Lloyd-Jones

"Congregational life wherein each member has his opportunity to contribute to the life of the whole body, those gifts with which the spirit endows him, is as much of the essence of the church as are ministry and sacraments."

— Bishop Lesslie Newbigin

"It is not the business of the church to adapt Christ to men, but men to Christ."

— Dorothy Sayers

"The church that is not jealousy protected by mighty intercession and sacrificial labors, will before long, become the abode of every evil bird and the hiding place for unsuspected corruption. The creeping wilderness will soon take over that church; that trusts in its own strength and forgets to watch and pray."

— A.W. Tozer

"The true church can never fail. For it is based upon a rock."

— T.S. Eliot

"I want the whole Christ for my Saviour, the whole Bible for my book, the whole church for my fellowship, and the whole world for my mission field."

— John Wesley

"The perfect church service would be one we were almost unaware of. Our attention would have been on God."

— C.S. Lewis

"What if every church was a church planting church?"

— John Van Pay

Maxims

- There are no little people, no little places.
- Love finds a need and meets it.
- The church doesn't need you; you need the church.

- Rules without relationship lead to rebellion.
- Something must be loved before it becomes loveable.
- Someone must be loved before it becomes loveable.

Discussion Questions

1) What's the vision and mission of your local church?
2) Why is community essential for a believer's maturity and evangelism?
3) How does the church pursue, provide and protect the flock of God?

Practical Challenges

1) Volunteer to help wherever you are needed, and remain there until you train your replacement.
2) Study the history of your church. (You will see the faithfulness of God.)
3) If you're not in fellowship, join a small group quickly. If your not generous, consistently give to God. If your not serving, then serve.

Further Study

The Church in God, Harold J. Ockenga
The Christian Manifesto, Francis Schaeffer
How Should We Then Live?, Francis Schaeffer
Ships of Pearl (First Bride), F.W. Boreham
Destined for the Throne, Paul Billheimer
Streams of Living Water, Richard Foster
The Ministry of the Word, G. Campbell Morgan
The Westminster Pulpit, G. Campbell Morgan
The Master Plan of Evangelism, Robert E. Coleman
The Master Plan of Discipleship, Robert E. Coleman
Dry Bones Can Live Again, Robert E. Coleman
The Acts of the Apostles, G. Campbell Morgan
Father Make Us One, Floyd McClung
21 Century Reformation (PDF), Winkie Pratney

The Taste of New Wine, Keith Miller
The New Testament Church (YouTube), David Pawson
The Father Heart of God, Floyd McClung, Jr.
Images of the Church in Mission, John Driver
Building Up One Another, Gene A. Getz
Systematic Theology Vol 3: Chapter 1, Ernest S. Williams
Youth Aflame ("James the Lesser" chapter), Winkie Pratney
The Complete Works of Francis Schaeffer: Vol. 4: A Christian View of the Church
The Complete Works of Francis Schaeffer: Vol. 5: A Christian View of the West

CHAPTER 11: SPIRITUAL AUTHORITY

The Gospel came not to an individual but to a community, to a place of safety and oversight, to a band of brothers and sisters trusting God and trusting each other. Nothing is so contrary to the heart of rebellious men than God's authority. Selfishness, the rotten fruit of pride and rebellion, constantly pushes man to a place of self-preservation and self-reliance. In contrast, in the kingdom of God, sacrifice and surrender are its cardinal ethics, in which Christ in others is trusted more than oneself.

Scripture

Ephesians 5:21
> "Submitting to one another in the fear of God."

Philippians 2:3
> "Let nothing be done through selfish ambition or conceit, but in lowliness of mind let each esteem others better than himself."

1 Corinthians 16:16
> "That you also submit to such, and to everyone who works and labors with us."

Hebrews 13:17
> "Obey those who rule over you, and be submissive, for they watch out for your souls, as those who must give account. Let them do so with joy and not with grief, for that would be unprofitable for you."

Matthew 8:5–13
> "Now when Jesus had entered Capernaum, a centurion came to Him, pleading with Him, saying, 'Lord, my servant is lying at home paralyzed, dreadfully tormented." And Jesus said to

him, "I will come and heal him.' The centurion answered and said, "Lord, I am not worthy that You should come under my roof. But only speak a word, and my servant will be healed. "For I also am a man under authority, having soldiers under me. And I say to this one, "Go," and he goes; and to another, "Come," and he comes; and to my servant, "Do this," and he does it.' When Jesus heard it, He marveled, and said to those who followed, 'Assuredly, I say to you, I have not found such great faith, not even in Israel!' And I say to you that many will come from east and west, and sit down with Abraham, Isaac, and Jacob in the kingdom of heaven. 'But the sons of the kingdom will be cast out into outer darkness. There will be weeping and gnashing of teeth.' Then Jesus said to the centurion, 'Go your way; and as you have believed, so let it be done for you.' And his servant was healed that same hour."

1 Peter 5:5

"Likewise you younger people, submit yourselves to your elders. Yes, all of you be submissive to one another, and be clothed with humility, for "God resists the proud, But gives grace to the humble."

Romans 13:1-6

"Let every soul be subject to the governing authorities. For there is no authority except from God, and the authorities that exist are appointed by God. Therefore whoever resists the authority resists the ordinance of God, and those who resist will bring judgment on themselves. For rulers are not a terror to good works, but to evil. Do you want to be unafraid of the authority? Do what is good, and you will have praise from the same. For he is God's minister to you for good. But if you do evil, be afraid; for he does not bear the sword in vain; for he is God's minister, an avenger to execute wrath on him who practices evil. Therefore you must be subject, not only because of wrath but also for conscience' sake. For because of this you also pay taxes, for they are God's ministers attending continually to this very thing."

Colossians 3:23–24

"And whatever you do, do it heartily, as to the Lord and not to men, knowing that from the Lord you will receive the reward of the inheritance; for you serve the Lord Christ."

1 Thessalonians 5:12–13

"And we urge you, brethren, to recognize those who labor among you, and are over you in the Lord and admonish you, and to esteem them very highly in love for their work's sake. Be at peace among yourselves."

Mark 9:35

"And He sat down, called the twelve, and said to them, "If anyone desires to be first, he shall be last of all and servant of all.""

The Necessity of Humility in a Christian's Walk

We must take upon ourselves the humility of Christ and make ourselves of no reputation. We must understand that we as a body of believers desperately need each other. Yielding and learning from each other's guidance, wisdom, and correction allows the Holy Spirit to flow through our relationships bringing forth His fruit and anointing.

The Necessity of Submission in a Christian's Walk

God has placed all authority, in our lives sovereignly. To understand this great truth is to walk in humility toward our leaders, bosses, pastors, parents and mentors. Remember we don't "have to submit to authority," we get to. It is for our own maturity and development as followers of Christ, that God has placed these individuals over us. We are to follow their example and yield to their guidance and instruction, for it is Christ in them, which is the true object of our loyalty and submission.

Quotes

"The Lord continued his teaching on the matter of authority. He called his disciples together and instructed them about future things in glory. He said that, among the gentiles, men seek for authority in order that they may rule over others. It is good for us to seek for the future glory, but we ought not have the thought of ruling or lording it over God's children. To do so would cause us to fall into the state of the gentiles. To exercise authority and to rule are the desires of the gentiles. Such a spirit must be driven from the church. Those whom the Lord uses are the ones who know the Lord's cup and the Lord's baptism."

— Watchman Nee

"God's purpose is that his children should look to him as their Father, and not to men. Perhaps I may suggest in passing that the reason for Christ's prohibition of the other two titles is substantially the same. We are not to be called 'rabbi,' posing as an authoritative teacher in our own right, nor 'master' as if we expected men to give us their slavish obedience. We are their 'slaves,' not they ours. The principal explanation of our Lord's categorical refusal to allow this kind of thing in the Christian church is that he saw in it an affront to God. God is our Father, Christ is our master, and (although this is not explicitly stated in the text) the Holy Spirit is our teacher. To set ourselves up, therefore, as the fathers, masters, and teachers of men is to usurp the glory of the eternal Trinity, and to arrogate to ourselves an authority over man which belongs to God alone."

— John R.W. Stott

"Don't be ashamed to learn from others."

— Girolamo Savonarola

"Carry the cross patiently, and with perfect submission; and in the end it shall carry you."

— Thomas à Kempis

"Authority exercised with humility, and obedience accepted with delight are the very lines along which our spirits live."

— C.S. Lewis

"The authority by which the Christian leader leads is not power but love, not force but example, not coercion but reasoned persuasion. Leaders have power, but power is safe only in the hands of those who humble themselves to serve."

— John R.W. Stott

"Shut up and grow up."

— Ravi Zacharias

"You will find, if you think for a moment, that the people who influence you are the people who believe in you."

— Henry Drummond

"Humility is the root, mother, nurse, foundation, and bond of all virtue."

— John Chrysostom

"The throne of God is established upon authority."

— Watchman Nee

Maxims

- We submit to Christ in people.
- Humility is a sober sense of reality.
- Rules without relationship always lead to rebellion.
- It is healthy to bow.
- Obedience is doing exactly what God says quickly, because you love him.
- Authority is never taken; it's always given.
- Authority is not a position but a disposition.
- Authority is a place to serve.
- Jesus doesn't want an audience but an army.

Discussion Questions

1) How important is a teachable heart in your Christian walk?
2) Do you take correction well? Is this important in Christian maturity?
3) What do you do if your leader sins against you?

Practical Challenges

1) Ask your spiritual mentor/leader where you can improve. Make action steps on how to practically improve.
2) Read Spiritual Authority by Watchman Nee.

Further Study

Spiritual Authority, Watchman Nee
A Tale of Three Kings, Gene Edwards
21st Century Reformation (PDF), Winkie Pratney
God's Armor Bearer, Terry Nance
Absolute Surrender, Andrew Murray
Celebration of Discipline, Richard Foster
Authority, Martyn Lloyd Jones
The Master Plan of Evangelism, Robert E. Coleman
The Master Plan of Discipleship, Robert E. Coleman
Spiritual Leadership, Oswald J. Sanders
The Imitation of Christ, Thomas à Kempis
Humility, Andrew Murray

CHAPTER 12: MIND IN LOVE WITH GOD

The mind in love with God is just that; it is a mind infatuated with his love and enamored by his presence. This sacred romance of the life of God in the soul of man has been and always will be a believer's refuge and spring. The thoughts of a person's mind can be an incomparable garden of beauty and worship to God or a desert of isolation, loneliness, and despair. Christians must cultivate this garden of their thoughts through the spiritual disciplines of meditation and prayer. *The reason there are so few speakers of God in the public is that there are so few thinkers about God in private.*

Scriptures

Deuteronomy 6:4–5

> "Hear, O Israel: The LORD our God, the LORD is one! "You shall love the LORD your God with all your heart, with all your soul, and with all your strength."

Matthew 22:36–38

> "Teacher, which is the great commandment in the law?" Jesus said to him, " 'You shall love the LORD your God with all your heart, with all your soul, and with all your mind.' This is the first and great commandment."

Romans 12:1–2

> "I beseech you therefore, brethren, by the mercies of God, that you present your bodies a living sacrifice, holy, acceptable to God, which is your reasonable service. And do not be conformed to this world, but be transformed by the renewing of your mind, that you may prove what is that good and acceptable and perfect will of God."

Philippians 2:5

> "Let this mind be in you which was also in Christ Jesus."

1 Corinthians 2:16

> "For "who has known the mind of the LORD that he may instruct Him?" But we have the mind of Christ."

Philippians 4:6–9

> "Be anxious for nothing, but in everything by prayer and supplication, with thanksgiving, let your requests be made known to God; and the peace of God, which surpasses all understanding, will guard your hearts and minds through Christ Jesus. Finally, brethren, whatever things are true, whatever things are noble, whatever things are just, whatever things are pure, whatever things are lovely, whatever things are of good report, if there is any virtue and if there is anything praiseworthy--meditate on these things. The things which you learned and received and heard and saw in me, these do, and the God of peace will be with you."

Romans 8:6

> "For to be carnally minded is death, but to be spiritually minded is life and peace."

Proverbs 23:7

> "For as he thinks in his heart, so is he. "Eat and drink!" he says to you, But his heart is not with you."

Colossians 3:2

> "Set your mind on things above, not on things on the earth."

Isaiah 26:3

> "You will keep him in perfect peace, Whose mind is stayed on You, Because he trusts in You."

Quotes

"The most important thing about a man is what he thinks about God."
— A.W. Tozer

"A soul is dyed by the color of its thoughts."

— Brother Daniel

"A state of mind that sees God in everything is evidence of growth in grace and a thankful heart."
— Charles G. Finney

"You are today where your thoughts about God have brought you."
— Brother Daniel

"We make our decisions, and then our decisions turn around and make us."
— F.W. Boreham

"Many Christians have so busied themselves with programs and activities that they no longer know how to be silent and meditate on God's word or recognize the mysteries that are in the person of Christ."
— Ravi Zacharias

"Fallacies do not cease to be fallacies because they become fashions."
— G.K. Chesterton

"The conscious mind determines the actions, the unconscious mind determines the reactions; and the reactions are just as important as the actions."
— E. Stanley Jones

"A thousand distractions would woo us away from thoughts of God, but if we are wise we will sternly put them from us and make room for the King and take time to entertain him."
— A.W. Tozer

"In order to know God, we must often think of him; and when we come to love him, we shall then also think of him often, for our heart will be with our treasure."
— Brother Lawrence

Maxims

- What is your life's integration point?
- Thoughts are to the soul what the bones are to the body.
- We fight with attitudes and ideas.
- A glass can only spill what it contains.
- Every day, prepare like you're going to preach to a thousand people.
- What does your relaxed mind default to?
- Thoughts lead to actions, actions become habits, habit becomes character, and character determines destiny.

Discussion Questions

1) What does your unengaged mind default back too? What does it take for this to be intimacy with Christ?
2) Why are biographies of Godly men and women indispensible to the Christian?
3) What is a sanctified imagination?

Practical Challenges

1) Fast from all media for a week.
2) Use Post-it notes as abiding reminders; place them around your life (car, shower, work, etc.).
3) Begin to take good, clear, concise notes over sermons and lectures.
4) Begin building your library, ask five people you respect in the faith their favorite Christian book, then buy it and read it.

Further Study

The Complete Works of F.W.Boreham
The Knowledge of the Holy, A.W. Tozer
My Pilgrimage, F.W. Boreham
The Chronicles of Narnia, C.S. Lewis
The Lord of the Rings, J.R.R. Tolkien

Practicing the Presence of God, Brother Lawrence
The Nature and Character of God, Winkie Pratney
Discovering the Character of God, George MacDonald
Knowing the Heart of God, George MacDonald
The Life of God in the Soul of Man, Henry Scougal
The Pursuit of God, A.W. Tozer
Orthodoxy, G.K. Chesteron
Paradise Lost, John Milton
The Thomas Factor, Winkie Pratney
In Two Minds, Os Guinness
Mere Christianity, C.S. Lewis
Spiritual Depression: It's Causes and its Cure, Martyn Lloyd Jones

CHAPTER 13: HOLINESS

Holiness is not the way to salvation, but rather, the fruit and character of salvation. A life transformed by the power of the Gospel and the grace of God should bear those eternal marks and reflect the beauty of his holiness. Just as Jesus in the days of His flesh pressed into the presence of the Father and always did what was pleasing to him, so must we press into more of Jesus, more of his Spirit, and more of his love. The maturity of a believer's walk is the purpose of the cross. The power of the resurrection fulfills his purpose, through our trust and obedience to him.

Scriptures

Matthew 5:48

> "Therefore you shall be perfect, just as your Father in heaven is perfect."

Hebrews 12:14

> "Pursue peace with all people, and holiness, without which no one will see the Lord."

Galatians 4:19

> "My little children, for whom I labor in birth again until Christ is formed in you."

Titus 2:11–12

> "For the grace of God that brings salvation has appeared to all men, teaching us that, denying ungodliness and worldly lusts, we should live soberly, righteously, and godly in the present age."

1 John 4:17

> "Love has been perfected among us in this: that we may have boldness in the day of judgment; because as He is, so are we in this world."

Psalm 15:1–5

"LORD, who may abide in Your tabernacle? Who may dwell in Your holy hill? He who walks uprightly, And works righteousness, And speaks the truth in his heart; He who does not backbite with his tongue, Nor does evil to his neighbor, Nor does he take up a reproach against his friend; In whose eyes a vile person is despised, But he honors those who fear the LORD; He who swears to his own hurt and does not change; He who does not put out his money at usury, Nor does he take a bribe against the innocent. He who does these things shall never be moved."

Psalm 24:1–5

"The earth is the LORD's, and all its fullness, The world and those who dwell therein. For He has founded it upon the seas, And established it upon the waters. Who may ascend into the hill of the LORD? Or who may stand in His holy place? He who has clean hands and a pure heart, Who has not lifted up his soul to an idol, Nor sworn deceitfully. He shall receive blessing from the LORD, And righteousness from the God of his salvation."

Luke 1:74–75

"To grant us that we, Being delivered from the hand of our enemies, Might serve Him without fear, In holiness and righteousness before Him all the days of our life."

1 Peter 1:15–16

"But as He who called you is holy, you also be holy in all your conduct, because it is written, "Be holy, for I am holy.""

2 Corinthians 7:1

"Therefore, having these promises, beloved, let us cleanse ourselves from all filthiness of the flesh and spirit, perfecting holiness in the fear of God."

Psalm 29:2

> "Give unto the LORD the glory due to His name; Worship the LORD in the beauty of holiness."

Romans 6:19

> "I speak in human terms because of the weakness of your flesh. For just as you presented your members as slaves of uncleanness, and of lawlessness leading to more lawlessness, so now present your members as slaves of righteousness for holiness."

Romans 8:29

> "For whom he did foreknow, he also did predestinate to be conformed to the image of his Son, that he might be the firstborn among many brethren."

Acts 24:16

> "This being so, I myself always strive to have a conscience without offense toward God and men."

Biblical Definitions and Descriptions of Holiness

Sincerity: The biblical idea regarding sincerity is that a believer's life is pure inside and out. The term arises from ancient times in regards to sculpting. An artist who had a crack in his sculpture would fill the cracks with a blend of crushed marble and wax. This fix would only last temporarily, as the sunlight would reveal the weakness—shining through the transparencies in the wax before melting it. In the same way, the Christian ideal is that our lives and devotions, when held up to the light of Christ, present no cracks or attempts to conceal.

Maturity: Maturity in life is defined as living up to the light or knowledge you have received at a given time. Reaching full development and maturity in the Christian faith is progressive, and yet at the same time, complete. Christian knowledge and understanding is always increasing, but obedience and faithfulness is either on or off. We grow in the grace of the Lord from glory to glory and faith to faith, but a Christian is always obedient to what he knows as he continues to learn.

Blamelessness: Blamelessness is a concept of intention. Sin is a premeditated, deliberate choice, where the caution and wisdom of God's law is completely disregarded. God in his infinite wisdom is able to see the intentions and motivations of our hearts and knows whether we are blameless or not.

Quotes

"Character in a saint means the disposition of Jesus Christ persistently manifested."

— Oswald Chambers

"Love is the foundation of all obedience."

— Alexander Maclaren

"There are two kinds of people in the world—only two kinds. Not black or white, rich or poor, but those either dead in sin or dead to sin."

— Leonard Ravenhill

"Nowhere can we get to know the holiness of God, and come under his influence and power, except in the inner chamber. It has been well said: 'no man can expect to make progress in holiness who is not often and long alone with God."

— Andrew Murray

"The gospel does not save whom it does not sanctify."

— Charles G. Finney

"Intelligence is good, obedience is mandatory, you can all be faithful."

— John Koeshall

"God never gives a command, without also giving the provision."

— W.K. Volkmer

"'Whosoever is born of God doth not commit sin; for his seed remaineth in him and he cannot sin, because he is born of God,' verse 9. But some men will say, 'true: whosoever is born of God doth not commit sin habitually.' Habitually! Whence is that? I read did not. It is not written in the book. God plainly saith, 'he doth not commit sin:' and thou addest habitually! Who art thou that mendest the oracles of God?—that 'addest to the words of this book?' Beware, I beseech thee, lest God, 'add to thee all the plagues that are written therein!'"

— John Wesley

"To become Christ-like is the only thing in the whole world worth caring for, the thing before which every ambition of man is folly and all lower achievement vain."

— Henry Drummond

"If thou bear the cross cheerfully, it will bear thee."

— Thomas à Kempis

"Sanctification does not depend as much on changing your activities as it does on doing them for God rather than for ourselves. Never tire of doing even the smallest things for him, because he isn't impressed so much with the dimensions of our work as with the love in which it is done."

— Brother Lawrence

"Look where you want to go."

— Eli Stewart

"The image of Christ that is forming within us—that is life's one charge. Let every project stand aside for that. 'till Christ be formed,' no man's work is finished, no religion crowned, no life has fulfilled its end."

— Henry Drummond

"Sin does not leap upon us fully armed. It steals in through a look, a swift, silent suggestion or imagination, but love and loyalty to Jesus will make you watchful and swift to rise up and cast out the subtle enemy. Do this and you shall live, and live victoriously."

— Samuel Logan Brengle

"The power comes from the pressing in, the striving for more, an insatiable desire for more of Him."

— W.K. Volkmer

"Holiness is not the way to salvation; it's the fruit and character of salvation."

— W.K. Volkmer

"All for Jesus! All for Jesus!
All my being's ransom'd pow'rs;
All my thoughts and words and doings,
All my days and all my hours.
All for Jesus! All for Jesus!
All my days and all my hours.
Let my hands perform his bidding;
Let my feet run in his ways;
      Let my eyes see Jesus only;
      Let my lips speak forth his praise.
      All for Jesus! All for Jesus!
      Let my lips speak forth his praise."

— Mary D. James

Maxims

- Meekness is not weakness, but rather, yielded strength.
- Holiness is wholeness.
- Holiness is sincerity.
- Holiness is blamelessness.
- Holiness is maturity.
- God holds you accountable for what you know.
- God never gives a command without also giving the provision.

Discussion Questions

1) Why is our culture more afraid of the doctrines of holiness than the presence of sin?
2) What is the expulsive power of a greater affection?
3) Can you be ninety five percent faithful to Christ?

Practical Challenges

1) Fast. (Nothing will bring greater sensitivity to the spirit; one-day/ three-day /five-day.)
2) Study the holiness of God. (Record the scriptures you find.)

Further Study

The God They Never Knew (Chapter 2), George Otis, Jr.
Helps to Holiness, Samuel Logan Brengle
The Principles of Holiness, Charles G. Finney
Victory over the World, Charles G. Finney
Systematic Theology, Charles G. Finney
Marked Reference Bible, J. Gilchrist Lawson
The Natural Ability of Man, Jesse Morrell
The Way of Holiness, Samuel Logan Brengle
Spiritual Lesson (Chapter 9), J. Oswald Sanders
Holiness and Power, A.M. Hills
Bible Readings on Holiness, Basil Miller
Holiness Manual & The Seven Overcomeths, George D. Watson
His Deeper Work in Us, J. Sidlow Baxter
Our Higher Calling, J. Sidlow Baxter
A New Call to Holiness, J. Sidlow Baxter
The General Next to God, Richard Collier
A Clear Account of Christian Perfection, John Wesley
Be Perfect, Andrew Murray
Limitations of Liberty, G. Campbell Morgan
Walking in the Spirit, George E. (Jed) Smock
Holy in Christ, Andrew Murray
Youth Aflame: A Manual for Discipleship, Winkie Pratney

CHAPTER 14: THE MINISTRY

The Commission of King Jesus is our marching orders to make disciples of all nations. This great campaign is being accomplished through proclamation and service. Once beachheads have been established into local churches and fellowships, these bodies will thrive and flourish through ministry unto the Lord. God has called us to steward these communities of worship, prayer, fellowship, discipleship, and witness. These communities exists to proclaim the gospel, train leaders, and engage in the mission of God as far as the ends of the earth until Christ's great campaign is accomplished.

Five Elements of Christian Community

Worship

Whether corporate or private, worship is ultimately a declaration that intimacy with Jesus is the most valuable thing in the universe.

Psalm 100:1–3
> "Make a joyful shout to the LORD, all you lands! Serve the LORD with gladness; Come before His presence with singing. Know that the LORD, He is God; It is He who has made us, and not we ourselves; We are His people and the sheep of His pasture."

Psalm 98:1
> "Oh, sing to the LORD a new song! For He has done marvelous things; His right hand and His holy arm have gained Him the victory."

Prayer

We must maintain both private devotion and intercession to advance the kingdom of God in our hearts and ministries.

1 Thessalonians 5:17
> "Pray without ceasing."

2 Chronicles 7:14

> "If My people who are called by My name will humble themselves, and pray and seek My face, and turn from their wicked ways, then I will hear from heaven, and will forgive their sin and heal their land."

Fellowship

The gospel from its inception has flowed from and into communities; transforming cultures, countries and kingdoms in its wake. This fellowship must be protected, nourished and fought for and this is accomplished through our love and devotion to each other.

1 John 1:7

> "But if we walk in the light as He is in the light, we have fellowship with one another, and the blood of Jesus Christ His Son cleanses us from all sin."

Hebrews 10:25

> "Not forsaking the assembling of ourselves together, as is the manner of some, but exhorting one another, and so much the more as you see the Day approaching."

Discipleship / Training Leaders

Discipleship is taking spiritual responsibility for others until they also take spiritual responsibility for other people. This trans-generational movement is the divine method of Jesus, which he practiced, beginning on the shores of Galilee.

John 13:15

> "For I have given you an example, that you should do as I have done to you."

Matthew 28:18–20

> "And Jesus came and spoke to them, saying, "All authority has been given to Me in heaven and on earth. "Go therefore and make disciples of all the nations, baptizing them in the

name of the Father and of the Son and of the Holy Spirit, "teaching them to observe all things that I have commanded you; and lo, I am with you always, even to the end of the age." Amen."

John 15:8

"By this My Father is glorified, that you bear much fruit; so you will be My disciples."

Witness

The greatest indicator of receiving the gospel, is the spreading of it in your life. Good news by its very nature spreads from house to house and heart to heart. We must realize you don't become a witness, you already are presently witnessing in your life to whatever is your supreme affection.

Acts 5:42

"And daily in the temple, and in every house, they did not cease teaching and preaching Jesus as the Christ."

Acts 4:33

"And with great power the apostles gave witness to the resurrection of the Lord Jesus. And great grace was upon them all."

1 John 1:2

"The life was manifested, and we have seen, and bear witness, and declare to you that eternal life which was with the Father and was manifested to us."

The Work of the Ministry

Proclamation

Like the apostles who came before us, we have received the same burden of the Lord to proclaim the salvation of Jesus to the watching world. Our message: Repentance and faith in Jesus Christ.

Mark 16:15

> "And He said to them, "Go into all the world and preach the gospel to every creature."

Luke 24:47

> "And that repentance and remission of sins should be preached in His name to all nations, beginning at Jerusalem."

Colossians 1:28

> "Him we preach, warning every man and teaching every man in all wisdom, that we may present every man perfect in Christ Jesus."

Acts 2:38

> "Then Peter said to them, "Repent, and let every one of you be baptized in the name of Jesus Christ for the remission of sins; and you shall receive the gift of the Holy Spirit."

Training Leaders / Discipleship

Essential to the advancement of the kingdom of God is more laborers in the harvest. Men and women must be brought to maturity in the faith and thoroughly equipped for every good work.

2 Timothy 2:2

> "And the things that you have heard from me among many witnesses, commit these to faithful men who will be able to teach others also."

1 Corinthians 11:1

> "Imitate me, just as I also imitate Christ."

2 Timothy 3:14

> "But you must continue in the things which you have learned and been assured of, knowing from whom you have learned them."

Mission

God's war for the souls of mankind has raged since the exile from Eden. The Father's accomplishment through the Son's triumph of the cross has secured the offer of salvation to all peoples, tribes, and tongues. The redeemed now collectively bear this responsibility and privilege to declare to the nations the gospel.

Mark 10:45

> "For who is greater, he who sits at the table, or he who serves? Is it not he who sits at the table? Yet I am among you as the One who serves."

Luke 22:27

> "For who is greater, he who sits at the table, or he who serves? Is it not he who sits at the table? Yet I am among you as the One who serves."

John 13:3–5

> "Jesus, knowing that the Father had given all things into His hands, and that He had come from God and was going to God, rose from supper and laid aside His garments, took a towel and girded Himself. After that, He poured water into a basin and began to wash the disciples' feet, and to wipe them with the towel with which He was girded."

Quotes

"We are therefore Christ's ambassadors, as though God were making his appeal through us. We implore you on Christ's behalf: be reconciled to God. God made him who had no sin to be sin for us, so that in him we might become the righteousness of God."

— The Apostle Paul

"Every student goes, every students gives, every student prays, every student welcomes."

— E. Scott Martin

"If you would serve the King, cross the line."

— Eli Gautreaux

"A few people so dedicated in time will shake the world for God. Victory is never won by the multitudes."

— Robert E. Coleman

"Show me your vision and I'll show you your future."

— E. Scott Martin

"We talk of the second coming when half of the world has not heard of the first."

— Oswald J. Smith

"It is good to tell people what we mean, but it is infinitely better to show them. People are looking for a demonstration, not an explanation."

— Robert E. Coleman

"If you want a friend, be a friend. Lord, help me make a friend today."

— Jonathan Bryce

"If we abandon the evangelization of the college campus we abandon America."

— Christopher G. Smith

"Nothing is ever really yours until you share it."

— E. Stanley Jones

Maxims

- Find, feed, and fight for the lambs of God.
- Make disciples. Make disciples. Make disciples.
- If you want a friend, be a friend.
- What God does in you he wants to do through you.

- Transforming the University, the Marketplace, and the World.
- Hunger, Humility, and Honor.
- Gathered for a season scattered for a lifetime.
- Pursue, provide, and protect the flock of God.
- Finish the race.
- Helping friends become devoted followers of Jesus.

Discussion Questions

1) What is your role in developing a culture of honor in your ministry?
2) What are the consequences of a ministry not training leaders?
3) Can a Christian community exist without (Any of the five elements of Christian community)?

Practical Challenges

1) Ask your spiritual mentor/ small group leader, "Why do you do the things you do?" (Respectfully)
2) Memorize your ministry's mission statement.

Further Study

Discipleship by Design, Harvey Herman
Live Dead Journal, Dick Brogden
Building Up One Another, Gene A. Getz
The Westminster Pulpit, G. Campbell Morgan
The Complete Works of Frank William Boreham
The Complete Works of Louis Albert Banks
Habitudes, Dr. Tim Elmore and Harvey Herman
Master Plan of Evangelism, Robert E. Coleman
Master Plan of Discipleship, Robert E. Coleman
Something Beautiful for God, Malcolm Muggeridge
The Lost Art of Discipleship, Leroy Eims
The Training of the Twelve, A.B. Bruce
Spiritual Leadership, J. Oswald Sanders
Shoe Leather Commitment, J. Oswald Sanders

Chapter 14: The Ministry

Youth Aflame, Winkie Pratney
Ultimate Core, Winkie Pratney
Marathon Faith, John Van Pay
God's Generals, Robert Liardon
The Ministry of the Word, G. Campbell Morgan

CHAPTER 15: WORSHIP

William Temple said, "Worship is to quicken the conscience by the holiness of God, to purge the imagination by the beauty of God, to open the heart to the love of God, and to devote the will to the purpose of God." It is also a warrior's weapon, a lover's song, a heart's devotion, a duty that becomes a delight, and finally, a paradise regained through praise and adoration. Whether corporate or private, worship is ultimately a declaration that intimacy with Jesus is the most valuable thing in the universe.

Scriptures

Matthew 4:10
> "Then Jesus said to him, "Away with you, Satan! For it is written, 'You shall worship the LORD your God, and Him only you shall serve."

John 4:23–24
> "But the hour is coming, and now is, when the true worshipers will worship the Father in spirit and truth; for the Father is seeking such to worship Him. "God is Spirit, and those who worship Him must worship in spirit and truth."

Colossians 3:16
> "Let the word of Christ dwell in you richly in all wisdom, teaching and admonishing one another in psalms and hymns and spiritual songs, singing with grace in your hearts to the Lord."

Psalm 66:4
> "All the earth shall worship You And sing praises to You; They shall sing praises to Your name." Selah

Psalm 105:1
> "Oh, give thanks to the LORD! Call upon His name; Make known His deeds among the peoples!"

Psalm 95:6

"Oh come, let us worship and bow down; Let us kneel before the LORD our Maker."

Psalm 22:3

"But You are holy, Enthroned in the praises of Israel."

Acts 24:14

"But this I confess to you, that according to the Way which they call a sect, so I worship the God of my fathers, believing all things which are written in the Law and in the Prophets."

Philippians 3:3

"For we are the circumcision, which worship God in the spirit, and rejoice in Christ Jesus, and have no confidence in the flesh."

Isaiah 6:1

"In the year that King Uzziah died, I saw the Lord sitting on a throne, high and lifted up, and the train of His robe filled the temple."

Revelation 5:9–10

"And they sang a new song, saying: "You are worthy to take the scroll, And to open its seals; For You were slain, And have redeemed us to God by Your blood Out of every tribe and tongue and people and nation, And have made us kings and priests to our God; And we shall reign on the earth."

Psalm 150:1–6

"Praise the LORD! Praise God in His sanctuary; Praise Him in His mighty firmament! Praise Him for His mighty acts; Praise Him according to His excellent greatness! Praise Him with the sound of the trumpet; Praise Him with the lute and harp! Praise Him with the timbrel and dance; Praise Him with stringed instruments and flutes! Praise Him with loud cymbals; Praise Him with clashing cymbals! Let everything that has breath praise the LORD. Praise the LORD!"

Psalm 46:10

"Be still, and know that I am God; I will be exalted among the nations, I will be exalted in the earth!"

Psalm 63:4

"Thus I will bless You while I live; I will lift up my hands in Your name."

Psalm 149:3

"Let them praise His name with the dance; Let them sing praises to Him with the timbrel and harp."

Quotes

"O come all ye faithful
Joyful and triumphant,
O come ye, o come ye to Bethlehem.
Come and behold him,
Born the king of angels;
O come, let us adore him,
O come, let us adore him,
O come, let us adore him,
Christ the Lord."

— John Wade

"To worship is to quicken the conscience by the holiness of God, to purge the imagination by the beauty of God, to open the heart to the love of God, and to devote the will to the purpose of God."

— William Temple

"Should I worship him from fear of hell, may I be cast into it. Should I serve him from desire of gaining heaven, may he keep me out. But should I worship him from love alone, he reveals himself to me, that my whole heart may be filled with his love and presence."

— Sadhu Sundar Singh

"We're here to be worshippers first and workers only second. We take a convert and immediately make a worker out of him. God never meant it to be so. God meant that a convert should learn to be a worshiper, and after that he can learn to be a worker…the work done by a worshiper will have eternity in it."

— A.W. Tozer

"To worship God in truth is to recognize him for being who he is, and to recognize ourselves for what we are."

— Brother Lawrence

"Worshippers aren't made when they see the enemy on the run, put to flight. The truth is worshippers of God are made during dark, stormy nights. And how we respond to our storms determines just what kind of worshippers we are."

— David Wilkerson

"For the Christian, worship is co-extensive with life. Life is already an expression of worship."

— Ravi Zacharias

"Adoration is the spontaneous yearning of the heart to worship, honour, magnify, and bless God. We ask nothing but to cherish him. We seek nothing but his exaltation. We focus on nothing but his goodness."

— Richard J. Foster

"To gather with God's people in united adoration of the Father is as necessary to the people as prayer."

— Martin Luther

"I've come to bow down to worship, to clothe you in worth, I've come to offer my life again, in my act of sacrifice, I don't come based on anything that I've done, only through your finished work on the cross."

— James Rey

Maxims

- The chief end of man is to glorify God and enjoy him forever.
- You become like the God you worship.
- "Worth-ship." We attribute worth and value to the person of God.
- Man was made to worship. You will worship something.
- The conviction of worship is that you choose to worship.
- Our heart will follow our posture.
- You're as close to God as you want to be.
- The first step away from God is ingratitude.
- The will is king, and emotions are its servants.

Discussion Questions

1) Why is God worthy of worship?
2) How can we cultivate a life style of worship?
3) What does it mean that we are worshippers first, workers second?

Practical Challenges

1) Study and implement the different methods of worship. (Try a method that isn't instinctual to your personality.)
2) Discover the worship of giving.

Further Study

Spiritual Lessons (Chapter 11), J. Oswald Sanders
The Treasury of David, Charles Spurgeon
The Knowledge of the Holy, A.W. Tozer
The Christian Book of Mystical Verse, A.W. Tozer
Whatever Happened to Worship, A.W. Tozer
The Way, E. Stanley Jones

Chapter 15: Worship

Abide in Christ, Andrew Murray
The Practice of the Presence of God, Brother Lawrence
Celebrations of Discipline (Chapters 11 & 13), Richard Foster
The Philosophy of the Plan of Salvation, James B. Walker
For All God's Worth: True Worship and the Calling of the Church, N.T.
    Wright

CHAPTER 16: PRAYER

Prayer in its essence is communion with God—a real communion to the Father, through the Son, by the Spirit. A failure of prayer is primarily a resistance to start. For only in the presence of Jesus, are our eyes enthralled by his beauty, our minds captivated by his wonder, our ears attuned to his stillness, and our hearts sensitive to his touch. *Oh taste and see that the Lord is good.*

Scriptures

John 14:13

> "And whatever you ask in My name, that I will do, that the Father may be glorified in the Son."

Matthew 6:5–13

> "And when you pray, you shall not be like the hypocrites. For they love to pray standing in the synagogues and on the corners of the streets, that they may be seen by men. Assuredly, I say to you, they have their reward. "But you, when you pray, go into your room, and when you have shut your door, pray to your Father who is in the secret place; and your Father who sees in secret will reward you openly. "And when you pray, do not use vain repetitions as the heathen do. For they think that they will be heard for their many words. "Therefore do not be like them. For your Father knows the things you have need of before you ask Him. "In this manner, therefore, pray: Our Father in heaven, Hallowed be Your name. Your kingdom come. Your will be done On earth as it is in heaven. Give us this day our daily bread. And forgive us our debts, As we forgive our debtors. And do not lead us into temptation, But deliver us from the evil one. For Yours is the kingdom and the power and the glory forever. Amen."

James 4:2–3

"You lust and do not have. You murder and covet and cannot obtain. You fight and war. Yet you do not have because you do not ask. You ask and do not receive, because you ask amiss, that you may spend it on your pleasures."

Philippians 4:6
> "Be anxious for nothing, but in everything by prayer and supplication, with thanksgiving, let your requests be made known to God."

Matthew18:19–20
> "Again I say to you that if two of you agree on earth concerning anything that they ask, it will be done for them by My Father in heaven. "For where two or three are gathered together in My name, I am there in the midst of them."

Luke 18:10–14
> "Two men went up to the temple to pray, one a Pharisee and the other a tax collector. "The Pharisee stood and prayed thus with himself, 'God, I thank You that I am not like other men-- extortioners, unjust, adulterers, or even as this tax collector. 'I fast twice a week; I give tithes of all that I possess.' "And the tax collector, standing afar off, would not so much as raise his eyes to heaven, but beat his breast, saying, 'God, be merciful to me a sinner!' "I tell you, this man went down to his house justified rather than the other; for everyone who exalts himself will be humbled, and he who humbles himself will be exalted."

1 John 5:14–15
> "Now this is the confidence that we have in Him, that if we ask anything according to His will, He hears us. And if we know that He hears us, whatever we ask, we know that we have the petitions that we have asked of Him."

Matthew 7:7–8
> "Ask, and it will be given to you; seek, and you will find; knock, and it will be opened to you. "For everyone who asks

receives, and he who seeks finds, and to him who knocks it will be opened."

James 1:5–8

"If any of you lacks wisdom, let him ask of God, who gives to all liberally and without reproach, and it will be given to him. But let him ask in faith, with no doubting, for he who doubts is like a wave of the sea driven and tossed by the wind. For let not that man suppose that he will receive anything from the Lord; he is a double-minded man, unstable in all his ways."

John 17:1–26

"Jesus spoke these words, lifted up His eyes to heaven, and said: "Father, the hour has come. Glorify Your Son, that Your Son also may glorify You, "as You have given Him authority over all flesh, that He should give eternal life to as many as You have given Him. "And this is eternal life, that they may know You, the only true God, and Jesus Christ whom You have sent. "I have glorified You on the earth. I have finished the work which You have given Me to do. "And now, O Father, glorify Me together with Yourself, with the glory which I had with You before the world was. "I have manifested Your name to the men whom You have given Me out of the world. They were Yours, You gave them to Me, and they have kept Your word. "Now they have known that all things which You have given Me are from You. "For I have given to them the words which You have given Me; and they have received them, and have known surely that I came forth from You; and they have believed that You sent Me. "I pray for them. I do not pray for the world but for those whom You have given Me, for they are Yours. "And all Mine are Yours, and Yours are Mine, and I am glorified in them. "Now I am no longer in the world, but these are in the world, and I come to You. Holy Father, keep through Your name those whom You have given Me, that they may be one as We are. "While I was with them in the world, I kept them in Your name. Those whom You gave Me I have kept; and none of them is lost except the son of perdition, that the Scripture might be fulfilled. "But now I come to You, and these things I speak in the world, that they may have My joy fulfilled in themselves. "I have given them Your word; and the world has hated them because they are not of the world, just as I am not of the world. "I do not pray that You should take them out of the world, but that You should keep them from the evil one. "They are not of the world, just as I am not of the world. "Sanctify them by Your truth. Your word is truth. "As You sent Me into the world, I also have sent them into the world. "And for their sakes I sanctify Myself, that they also may be sanctified by the truth. "I do not pray for these alone, but also for those who will believe in Me through their word; "that they all may be one, as You, Father, are in Me, and I in You; that they also may be one in Us, that the world may believe that You sent Me. "And the glory which You gave Me I have given them, that they may be one just as We are one: "I in them, and You in Me; that they may be made perfect in one, and that the world may know that You have sent Me, and have loved them as You have loved Me. "Father, I desire that they also whom You gave Me may be with Me where I am, that they may behold My glory which You have given Me; for You loved Me before the foundation of the world. "O righteous Father! The world has not known You, but I have known You; and these have known that You sent Me. "And I have declared to them Your name, and will declare it, that the love with which You loved Me may be in them, and I in them."

Jude 1:20

"But you, beloved, building yourselves up on your most holy faith, praying in the Holy Spirit."

Ephesians 6:18

"Praying always with all prayer and supplication in the Spirit, being watchful to this end with all perseverance and supplication for all the saints."

Types of Prayer

Personal

Following in the footsteps of our Master, it doesn't take many steps to realize he prayed. Notice the cry of the disciples was not, "Teach us to preach to the multitudes" or "Teach us to heal the sick." They asked, *"Lord teach us to pray,"* for they knew that prayer was the source of Christ's courage and love, his power and wisdom.

Matthew 14:22–23
> "Immediately Jesus made His disciples get into the boat and go before Him to the other side, while He sent the multitudes away. And when He had sent the multitudes away, He went up on the mountain by Himself to pray. Now when evening came, He was alone there."

Corporate

Gathered together in agreement in prayer was where the birth of the Christian church took place. It was in corporate prayer long ago that the Spirit of God inflamed the hearts of the disciples in passion and adoration and equipped them with power to minister and preach. The body of Christ has been and will always be a body of believers unified in prayer to Christ.

Matthew 18:20
> "For where two or three are gathered together in My name, I am there in the midst of them."

Abiding

The wisdom of the saints and their most precious possession has always been the presence of Jesus. To remain aware of Christ's presence and the discipline of the heart toward constant communion with him is the believer's greatest joy and most severe responsibility. Christ's promise of intimacy to those who seek it is the uniqueness of the Christian message—*Christ in you the hope of glory.*

John 15:4

> "Abide in Me, and I in you. As the branch cannot bear fruit of itself, unless it abides in the vine, neither can you, unless you abide in Me."

Quotes

"No man is greater than his prayer life."

— Leonard Ravenhill

"God doesn't answer prayer but a desperate prayer."

— Leonard Ravenhill

"Prayer does not equip us for greater works—prayer is the greater work."

— Oswald Chambers

"A revival may be expected when Christians have a spirit of prayer for a revival. That is, when they pray as if their hearts were set upon it. When Christians have the spirit of prayer for a revival. When they go about groaning out their hearts desire. When they have real travail of soul."

— Charles G. Finney

"Talking to men for God is a great thing, but talking to God for men is greater still. He will never talk well and with real success to men for God who has not learned well how to talk to God for men."

— E. M. Bounds

"We need to remind ourselves that although prayer is a very personal and private communication with God, pouring out our repentance and sorrow for sin, it is also to be a constant connection with God, an unbroken communication, a means of receiving assurance as to how to go on in this next hour in our work, and our means of receiving guidance. Prayer is also to be our means of receiving sufficient grace and strength to do what we are being guided to do. This reality is to be handed to the next generation, not to end when we die."

— Edith Schaeffer

"There are many beautiful things in the world around us, but pearls can only be discovered in the depths of the sea; if we wish to possess spiritual pearls we must plunge into the depths, that is, we must pray, we must sink down into the secret depths of contemplation and prayer. Then we shall perceive precious pearls."

— Sadhu Sundar Singh

"God will do nothing but in answer to prayer."

— John Wesley

"If I throw out a boathook from the boat and catch hold of the shore and pull, do I pull the shore to me, or do I pull myself to the shore? Prayer is not pulling God to my will, but the aligning of my will to the will of God."

— E. Stanley Jones

"God's fighting for us does not exclude the responsibility to be prepared for battle both in the area of strategy and in equipment. Trusting God completely in prayer, believing that He is able to do all things, does not remove the need to pray for His strength to accomplish what He has prepared us to do! We are to do what He is unfolding for us to do, fulfilling what God is giving us strength to do, acknowledging that it is His strength and not ours. It is a truly active passive, not a false whining humbleness that says, 'I can't do anything; I'm too weak.'"

— Edith Schaeffer

"A sinning man stops praying but a praying man stops sinning."

— Leonard Ravenhill

Maxims

- Prayer is both a relationship to be experienced with God and a work to be done for God.
- Religion is a checklist; truth is a person.
- Prayer is going home.
- We can ask him what he is up to in the world and ask him how we can fit in with that.
- Who has ever regretted spending time with God?

Discussion Questions

1) How did Jesus model a lifestyle of prayer to the Father?
2) What's the greatest hindrance to your prayer life?
3) How do you develop a hunger for spiritual things in your self and in others?

Practical Challenges

1) Pray for one hour. (Start in twenty minute increments)
2) Pray for the nations of the world. (Buy a globe, map, or map shower curtain.)
3) Challenge your self to ask others "Is there anything you need prayer for?" Start by asking five a day.

Further Study

Rees Howell: Intercessor, Norman Grubb
Prevailing Prayer, Charles G. Finney
Practice in Prayer, G. Campbell Morgan
Live Dead Joy, Dick Brogden
Effective Prayer, J. Oswald Sanders
The Three Keys of Availing Prayer, Samuel Isenhower
Ministry of Intercession, Andrew Murray
With Christ in the School of Prayer, Andrew Murray
Complete Works on Prayer, E.M. Bounds
Revival Praying, Leonard Ravenhill

Why Revival Tarries, Leonard Ravenhill
Meat for Men, Leonard Ravenhill
Treasury of Prayer, Leonard *Ravenhill and E.M. Bounds*
Destined for the Throne, Paul Billheimer
If Ye Shall Ask, Oswald Chambers
Remarkable Incidents, G.C. Bevington
How to Pray, R.A. Torrey
Praying Clear Through, William J. Harney
The Fourth Dimension, Dr. David Yonggi Cho

CHAPTER 17: FELLOWSHIP

The resurrection of Jesus not only secured the way of salvation for mankind, but it also provided healing and restoration of true friendship for us. Jesus has shown us how to live and treat each other. Therefore, in following in his unselfishness, the miracle of fellowship is birthed. This fellowship and brotherhood must be protected and enhanced by mutually shared convictions and loving, unselfish service. This unity among a group of diverse believers is the greatest reflection of the beauty and majesty of the Trinity.

Scriptures

1 Corinthians 1:9

> "God is faithful, by whom you were called into the fellowship of His Son, Jesus Christ our Lord."

Acts 2:42–47

> "And they continued steadfastly in the apostles' doctrine and fellowship, in the breaking of bread, and in prayers. Then fear came upon every soul, and many wonders and signs were done through the apostles. Now all who believed were together, and had all things in common, and sold their possessions and goods, and divided them among all, as anyone had need. So continuing daily with one accord in the temple, and breaking bread from house to house, they ate their food with gladness and simplicity of heart, praising God and having favor with all the people. And the Lord added to the church daily those who were being saved."

John 17:20

> "I do not pray for these alone, but also for those who will believe in Me through their word."

Matthew 18:20

> "For where two or three are gathered together in My name, I am there in the midst of them."

Philippians 2:3

> "Let nothing be done through selfish ambition or conceit, but in lowliness of mind let each esteem others better than himself."

Galatians 6:1–2

> "Brethren, if a man is overtaken in any trespass, you who are spiritual restore such a one in a spirit of gentleness, considering yourself lest you also be tempted. Bear one another's burdens, and so fulfill the law of Christ."

Proverbs 18:1

> "A man who isolates himself seeks his own desire; He rages against all wise judgment."

The Four Convictions of Fellowship

Common Understanding

We as a body of believers are unified with a common purpose of advancing God's kingdom together with a unified mind. The mind of Christ contains a common understanding of the fundamentals of the Christian faith. This faith allows for a collective vision and purpose to proclaim his Gospel, train and entrust leaders, and to serve wholeheartedly, locally and abroad. We must maintain the discipline of majoring on majors and not allowing personal interpretations or traditions to distract us from Christ's mandate to preach, train, and serve.

Jude 1:3

> "Beloved, while I was very diligent to write to you concerning our common salvation, I found it necessary to write to you exhorting you to contend earnestly for the faith which was once for all delivered to the saints."

1 Corinthians 12:12–14

> "For as the body is one and has many members, but all the members of that one body, being many, are one body, so also

is Christ. For by one Spirit we were all baptized into one body--whether Jews or Greeks, whether slaves or free--and have all been made to drink into one Spirit. For in fact the body is not one member but many."

Amos 3:3

"Can two walk together, unless they are agreed?"

Common Unselfishness

The cost of true unity is that of self-denial. *Let every man consider others better than himself.* This humility allows the Spirit to reveal to our hearts the great need we have for others. This revelation from the Spirit to our hearts bears the fruit of unselfish love towards our brothers and sisters and releases the grip of greed and self-preservation. A cardinal ethic of Christianity has always been sacrifice.

Luke 9:24

"For whoever desires to save his life will lose it, but whoever loses his life for My sake will save it."

Galatians 5:13

"For you, brethren, have been called to liberty; only do not use liberty as an opportunity for the flesh, but through love serve one another."

Acts 2:44-45

"Now all who believed were together, and had all things in common, and sold their possessions and goods, and divided them among all, as anyone had need."

1 John 3:17

"But whoever has this world's goods, and sees his brother in need, and shuts up his heart from him, how does the love of God abide in him?"

Constant Forgiveness

The surest evidence one has received the love and forgiveness God as offered through the cross of Christ is that such a person demonstrates love and forgiveness themselves. We become what we behold.

Matthew 18:21–22
> "Then Peter came to Him and said, "Lord, how often shall my brother sin against me, and I forgive him? Up to seven times?" Jesus said to him, "I do not say to you, up to seven times, but up to seventy times seven.""

Matthew 6:14–15
> "For if you forgive men their trespasses, your heavenly Father will also forgive you. "But if you do not forgive men their trespasses, neither will your Father forgive your trespasses."

Matthew 5:23–24
> "Therefore if you bring your gift to the altar, and there remember that your brother has something against you, "leave your gift there before the altar, and go your way. First be reconciled to your brother, and then come and offer your gift."

Commitment

The miracle of fellowship will never embrace the transient or halfhearted. For only when a body of believers is rooted and grounded in love and commitment to each other, and ultimately to the King, does the miracle of fellowship appear. In this hour of consumerism and short-lived spirituality, we must commit to each other's highest good and work and serve if we are to see a harvest.

Matthew 10:32–33
> "Therefore whoever confesses Me before men, him I will also confess before My Father who is in heaven. "But whoever denies Me before men, him I will also deny before My Father who is in heaven."

Matthew 16:24–27

> "Then Jesus said to His disciples, "If anyone desires to come after Me, let him deny himself, and take up his cross, and follow Me. "For whoever desires to save his life will lose it, but whoever loses his life for My sake will find it. "For what profit is it to a man if he gains the whole world, and loses his own soul? Or what will a man give in exchange for his soul? "For the Son of Man will come in the glory of His Father with His angels, and then He will reward each according to his works."

Matthew 24:12–13

> "And because lawlessness will abound, the love of many will grow cold. "But he who endures to the end shall be saved."

Quotes

"Our love to God is measured by our everyday fellowship with others and the love it displays."

— Andrew Murray

"Every person matters to God."

— John Van Pay

"You never have to advertise a fire. Everyone comes running when there's a fire. Likewise, if your church is on fire, you will not have to advertise it. The community will already know it."

— Leonard Ravenhill

"Nothing tends more to cement the hearts of Christians than praying together. Never do they love one another so well as when they witness the outpouring of each other's hearts in prayer."

— Charles G. Finney

"Forgiving and being forgiven are two names for the same thing. The important thing is that a discord has been resolved."

— C.S. Lewis

"Let him who cannot be alone beware of community...Let him who is not in community beware of being alone...Each by itself has profound perils and pitfalls. One who wants fellowship without solitude plunges into the void of words and feelings, and the one who seeks solitude without fellowship perishes in the abyss of vanity, self-infatuation and despair."

— Dietrich Bonhoeffer

"To be a Christian means to forgive the inexcusable, because God has forgiven the inexcusable in you."

— C.S. Lewis

"Every cord that binds me to Christ also binds me to my brother, and I can't break with one without breaking with the other."

— E. Stanley Jones

"By trusting and stewarding the convictions of fellowship, we together create and cultivate a culture of honor that the Spirit of God is pleased to dwell in and work through."

— W.K. Volkmer

"We few, we happy few, we band of brothers; For he today that sheds his blood with me, shall be my brother..."

— William Shakespeare

Maxims

- Major on the majors; minor on the minors.
- Christianity is a relaxed love relationship with God.
- Find, feed, and fight for the lambs of God.
- If you want a friend, be a friend.
- Love believes the best.
- People usually forget what you say, but they will always remember how you treat them.
- Love and laughter plow hard hearts.
- Most people belong before they believe.
- Community speaks louder than arguments.
- We must steward the convictions of fellowship.

Discussion Questions

1) How do we develop a culture of honor in our ministry?

2) If we have unforgiveness in our heart towards another, are we robbing others of true fellowship?
3) Explain why commitment is essential to fruitfulness in the Christian life?

Practical Challenges

1) Give away something of yours to someone in your community. (The qualification is that it hurts to give away.)
2) Forgiveness: Pray for ten minutes; ask the Holy Spirit whom you have unforgiveness and bitterness towards. (If you don't forgive, stop reading until you do.)
3) Find a way to serve; take the form of a servant. (Wash dishes, cars, take out the trash, etc.)

Further Study

Life Together, Dietrich Bonhoeffer
The Greatest Thing in the World, Henry Drummond
The Incendiary Fellowship, Elton Trueblood
Spiritual Lessons, J. Oswald Sanders
Four Loves, C.S. Lewis
The Fellowship of the Ring, J. R. R. Tolkien
My Life, Helen Keller
Luggage of Life (Our Desert Islands), F.W. Boreham
L'Abri, Edith Schaeffer
Youth Aflame: A Manual for Discipleship, Winkie Pratney
Silver Shadow (Comrades), F.W. Boreham
The Seven Spirits, General William Booth
Building Up One Another, Gene A. Getz
The Master Plan of Discipleship, Robert E. Coleman
The Mark of a Christian, Francis Schaeffer

CHAPTER 18: DISCIPLESHIP

The greatest need of this country is disciples of Jesus. Churches are either shrinking, dying, or filled with uncommitted, undisciplined, and potentially false converts. These symptoms come from the same root issue: disobedience to Christ's command to make disciples. Disciples can't be mass-produced in a classroom or manufactured through seminary. Jesus's method of sacrificing and investing His time is still the only way in which disciples are handcrafted. The quality of direct spiritual investment into a faithful, available, and teachable individual has proven, time and time again, to be irreplaceable. Christendom has, throughout the centuries, trusted that Jesus was divine, and yet has quickly forgotten that His method was also divine. May we rekindle the old flames of sacrifice and devotion, and walk the old paths upon which our Master has trodden.

Scriptures

John 13:35
> "By this all will know that you are My disciples, if you have love for one another."

John 13:15
> "For I have given you an example, that ye should do as I have done to you."

2 Timothy 2:2
> "And the things that you have heard from me among many witnesses, commit these to faithful men who will be able to teach others also."

Philippians 4:9
> "The things which you learned and received and heard and saw in me, these do, and the God of peace will be with you."

Matthew 28:18–20

"And Jesus came and spoke to them, saying, "All authority has been given to Me in heaven and on earth. Go therefore and make disciples of all the nations, baptizing them in the name of the Father and of the Son and of the Holy Spirit, teaching them to observe all things that I have commanded you; and lo, I am with you always, even to the end of the age." Amen.

Real Responsibility

A sure sign of Christian maturity is when a believer's focus shifts from the health of their own spiritual walk to that of others. By following our Master's teaching, we lay our own life down for the sake of others. Through this conviction, new believers receive the guidance, love, and instruction that they need to grow to maturity.

John 20:21

"So Jesus said to them again, "Peace to you! As the Father has sent Me, I also send you."

Luke 12:48

"But he who did not know, yet committed things deserving of stripes, shall be beaten with few. For everyone to whom much is given, from him much will be required; and to whom much has been committed, of him they will ask the more."

Matthew 28:18

"And Jesus came and spoke to them, saying, "All authority has been given to Me in heaven and on earth.""

Mark 16:15

"And He said to them, "Go into all the world and preach the gospel to every creature.""

2 Timothy 1:13

"Hold fast the pattern of sound words which you have heard from me, in faith and love which are in Christ Jesus."

Real Devotional Life

The wisdom of Jesus rings true as he says, "You are my disciples if you continue in my word." Our greatest privilege and delight is to read and pray. These ancient, tested disciplines are the source of our intimacy with Christ.

John 15:4–5

"Abide in Me, and I in you. As the branch cannot bear fruit of itself, unless it abides in the vine, neither can you, unless you abide in Me. I am the vine, you are the branches. He who abides in Me, and I in him, bears much fruit; for without Me you can do nothing."

Matthew 22:36–39

"Teacher, which is the great commandment in the law?" Jesus said to him, " 'You shall love the LORD your God with all your heart, with all your soul, and with all your mind.' This is the first and great commandment. And the second is like it: 'You shall love your neighbor as yourself.'"

Proverbs 23:7

"For as he thinks in his heart, so is he. "Eat and drink!" he says to you, but his heart is not with you."

Romans 12:1–3

"I beseech you therefore, brethren, by the mercies of God, that you present your bodies a living sacrifice, holy, acceptable to God, which is your reasonable service. And do not be conformed to this world, but be transformed by the renewing of your mind, that you may prove what is that good and acceptable and perfect will of God. For I say, through the grace given to me, to everyone who is among you, not to think of himself more highly than he ought to think, but to think soberly, as God has dealt to each one a measure of faith."

Real Relationships

When remembering the apostle Paul, people always remember him as a larger than life hero of the faith. Paul, in their mind, was preaching the gospel to angry mobs, healing the sick, or pioneering countless churches in Asia Minor. Few remember him as a man of deep friendship, and yet at the close of most his epistles, the true revelation of his greatest strength is shown: *Greet Priscilla and Aquila, Epenetus, Stephanus, Fortunatus, Barnibas, Silas, Titus, Luke, and Timothy.* These "coworkers of the gospel," as he calls them, are his close friends.

John 13:34–35

> "A new commandment I give to you, that you love one another; as I have loved you, that you also love one another. By this all will know that you are My disciples, if you have love for one another."

Psalm 133:1

> "Behold, how good and how pleasant it is For brethren to dwell together in unity!"

Proverbs 27:17

> "As iron sharpens iron, so a man sharpens the countenance of his friend."

Quotes

"The heart of discipleship rests in gratitude and responsibility."

— Eli Gautreaux

"Christianity without discipleship is always Christianity without Christ."

— Dietrich Bonhoeffer

"God needs those who are ready to lay down their very lives to lead others into true soldiership and a true following of the crucified."
— Amy Carmichael

"A man of God takes responsibility for himself first, and then others."
— John R. Hauck

"Discipleship is adherence to Christ."
— Dietrich Bonhoeffer

"Cheap grace is the preaching of forgiveness without requiring repentance, baptism without church discipline, communion without confession, absolution without personal confession. Cheap grace is grace without discipleship, grace without the cross, grace without Jesus Christ."
— Dietrich Bonhoeffer

"I am sure that there is no place in the world where your message would not be enhanced by your making the place (whether tiny or large, a hut or a palace) orderly, artistic and beautiful with some form of creativity, some form of 'art.'"
— Edith Schaeffer

"Having called his men, Jesus made a practice of being with them. This was the essence of his training program—just letting his disciples follow him."
— Robert E. Coleman

"Discipleship is ultimately taking responsibility to what is close to the heart of God."
— Eli Gautreaux

"Preaching to the masses, although necessary, will never suffice in the work of preparing leaders for evangelism. Nor can occasional prayer meetings and training classes for Christian workers do this job. Building men and women is not that easy. It requires constant personal attention, much like a father gives to his children. This is something that no organization or class can ever do. Children are not raised by proxy. The example of Jesus would teach us that it can be done only by persons staying close to those whom they seek to lead."

— Robert E. Coleman

"Only a disciple can make a disciple."

— A.W. Tozer

"By serving others, one puts oneself in the position of a learner."

— John R. Hauck

"If you want a friend, be a friend."

— Brother Daniel

"Jesus said, 'Greater things of these you shall do…' Become a peace builder, a bridge builder, not a destroyer, and the way you do that is through friendships and relationships, and through authentic character."

— Ravi Zacharias

"No matter how high the powers of reason, no matter how deep the intellect, no one can discover God's secret messages without paying the cost of true discipleship."

— Winkie Pratney

"The cost of making a disciple is being one."

— John R. Hauck

"Our relationship with each other is the criterion the world uses to judge whether our message is truthful – Christian community is the final apologetic."

— Francis R. Schaeffer

"Discipleship happens best in the context of a relationship."

— John Van Pay

Maxims

- A disciple is a learner.
- Discipline your weakness.
- The fruit of a mature disciple is another disciple.
- Life begets life.
- Responsibility is the miracle growth.
- God doesn't call the qualified. He qualifies the called.
- What leaders do in moderation, followers will do in excess.
- Disciples are faithful, available and teachable.
- Disciples are handcrafted not mass produced.
- What God does in you, he wants to do through you.
- A Disciple loves, serves, and sacrifices.
- Discipleship is cultivated through honor, humility and hunger.
- Real devotional life, real relationships, and real responsibility.
- The Kingdom of God moves through friendships
- Equip, empower, envision

Discussion Questions

1) Why does 1% of the Church make disciples? What can we do to change this?
2) What is your weakness in area of the (Three R's), is it real responsibility? Real relationships? Real devotional life? How do we discipline the areas of our weakness?
3) What is exponential power of trans-generational discipleship?

Practical Challenges

1) Spiritual lineages: Write a chain of your discipleship down, call and thank each of these people. Thank them for their commitment to Christ. For instance: Eli > Josh > John > Billy > Craig > Fabio > Miguel > Connor > Eddie >Joe > Ryan > Mark > Josh >Thomas
2) Read *The Master Plan of Evangelism* by Robert E. Coleman.

Further Study

The Lost Art of Discipleship, Leroy Eims
The Training of the Twelve, A.B. Bruce
Youth Aflame: A Manual for Discipleship, Winkie Pratney
Discipleship, G. Campbell Morgan
The Master Plan of Evangelism, Robert E. Coleman
The Master Plan of Discipleship, Robert E. Coleman
Spiritual Leadership, J. Oswald Sanders
Spiritual Lesson, J. Oswald Sanders
Spiritual Maturity, J. Oswald Sanders
A Spiritual Clinic, J. Oswald Sanders
Discipleship by Design, Harvey A. Herman
Small Group University, Rev. Brad Lewis
Lead So Others Can Follow, James T. Bradford
The Cost of Discipleship, Dietrich Bonhoeffer
For Believers Only, J. Oswald Sanders
Shoe Leather Commitment, J. Oswald Sanders
A Handbook for Followers of Jesus, Winkie Pratney
The Great Omission, Dallas Willard
The Parable of the Father's Heart , G. Campbell Morgan
Design for Discipleship, The Navigators
The Complete Book of Discipleship, Bill Hull
Born to Reproduce, Dawson Trotman (Sermon)

CHAPTER 19: EVANGELISM

"The only reason why those born again of the Spirit are left in the world is that they may be His witnesses." — G. Campbell Morgan

The apostolic heart cry is Christ crucified and resurrected. This is the message of the kingdom. This is the power and glory of the Gospel. This is the good news, the incorruptible seed of God. When planted in a heart of faith and love, it grows into fruition. This transformed life is the fruit and reward of Christ's victory. This life cannot help but bear witness and testify to the accomplishment of Christ. The heart of evangelism is that of a loving, outward response to the work of Christ. In joining with the passion of the apostles, we collectively proclaim that we cannot help but speak about what we have seen and heard. In this darkened and wicked hour, our only hope is the burden of the Lord. This weight and severity of divine responsibility is only alleviated through the obedient, reverent proclamation of the Gospel. Paul the apostle understood this responsibility when he cried out, *"Woe is me if I preach not the gospel."*

Scriptures

Testimony

Your testimony is telling the story of what Jesus has done, is doing, and will continue doing for you. *"God has given us eternal life and eternal life is in his Son."* The most important part of a testimony is not the sin and failures of a past life, but rather a feature on the transformation of character through the power of the Gospel.

Proverbs 11:30
> "The fruit of the righteous is a tree of life, and he who wins souls is wise."

Revelation 12:11
> "And they overcame him by the blood of the Lamb and by the

word of their testimony, and they did not love their lives to the death."

2 Timothy 1:8

"Therefore do not be ashamed of the testimony of our Lord, nor of me His prisoner, but share with me in the sufferings for the gospel according to the power of God."

1 John 5:11

"And this is the testimony: that God has given us eternal life, and this life is in His Son."

1 Peter 3:15

"But sanctify the Lord God in your hearts, and always be ready to give a defense to everyone who asks you a reason for the hope that is in you, with meekness and fear."

Evangelism

The heart of evangelism is spreading the gospel both to individuals and to groups. We as men and women of God must develop the practiced skill of telling the story of Jesus of Nazareth and calling men and women to repentance and faith in Jesus Christ.

Luke 9:26

"For whoever is ashamed of Me and My words, of him the Son of Man will be ashamed when He comes in His own glory, and in His Father's, and of the holy angels."

Matthew 5:14–16

"You are the light of the world. A city that is set on a hill cannot be hidden. Nor do they light a lamp and put it under a basket, but on a lampstand, and it gives light to all who are in the house. Let your light so shine before men, that they may see your good works and glorify your Father in heaven."

John 4:39–42

"And many of the Samaritans of that city believed in Him
because of the word of the woman who testified, 'He told me
all that I ever did.' So when the Samaritans had come to Him,
they urged Him to stay with them; and He stayed there two
days. And many more believed because of His own word.
Then they said to the woman, "Now we believe, not because
of what you said, for we ourselves have heard Him and we
know that this is indeed the Christ, the Savior of the world."

Matthew 10:7

"And as you go, preach, saying, 'The kingdom of heaven is at
hand.'"

Proclamation

Proclamation is the heralding of the victory of the resurrection. Its
central message is that of a person, Christ Jesus; him crucified and
resurrected. Through the wisdom and power of God, the conviction of
sin, righteousness, and judgment will be accomplished by the Holy
Spirit. This is God's method of reaching the masses with the Good
News.

Romans 10:15–17

"And how shall they preach unless they are sent? As it is
written: 'How beautiful are the feet of those who preach the
gospel of peace, Who bring glad tidings of good things!' But
they have not all obeyed the gospel. For Isaiah says, 'LORD,
who has believed our report?' So then faith comes by hearing,
and hearing by the word of God."

Romans 1:16

"For I am not ashamed of the gospel of Christ, for it is the
power of God to salvation for everyone who believes, for the
Jew first and also for the Greek."

Luke 14:23

> "Then the master said to the servant, 'Go out into the highways and hedges, and compel *them* to come in, that my house may be filled."

Matthew 24:14

> "And this gospel of the kingdom will be preached in all the world as a witness to all the nations, and then the end will come."

1 Corinthians 1:21–28

> "For since, in the wisdom of God, the world through wisdom did not know God, it pleased God through the foolishness of the message preached to save those who believe. For Jews request a sign, and Greeks seek after wisdom; but we preach Christ crucified, to the Jews a stumbling block and to the Greeks foolishness, but to those who are called, both Jews and Greeks, Christ the power of God and the wisdom of God. Because the foolishness of God is wiser than men, and the weakness of God is stronger than men. For you see your calling, brethren, that not many wise according to the flesh, not many mighty, not many noble, are called. But God has chosen the foolish things of the world to put to shame the wise, and God has chosen the weak things of the world to put to shame the things which are mighty; and the base things of the world and the things which are despised God has chosen, and the things which are not, to bring to nothing the things that are."

1 Corinthians 2:1–16

> "And I, brethren, when I came to you, did not come with excellence of speech or of wisdom declaring to you the testimony of God. For I determined not to know anything among you except Jesus Christ and Him crucified. I was with you in weakness, in fear, and in much trembling. And my speech and my preaching were not with persuasive words of human wisdom, but in demonstration of the Spirit and of

power, that your faith should not be in the wisdom of men but in the power of God. However, we speak wisdom among those who are mature, yet not the wisdom of this age, nor of the rulers of this age, who are coming to nothing. But we speak the wisdom of God in a mystery, the hidden wisdom which God ordained before the ages for our glory, which none of the rulers of this age knew; for had they known, they would not have crucified the Lord of glory. But as it is written: "Eye has not seen, nor ear heard, Nor have entered into the heart of man The things which God has prepared for those who love Him." But God has revealed them to us through His Spirit. For the Spirit searches all things, yes, the deep things of God. For what man knows the things of a man except the spirit of the man which is in him? Even so no one knows the things of God except the Spirit of God. Now we have received, not the spirit of the world, but the Spirit who is from God, that we might know the things that have been freely given to us by God. These things we also speak, not in words which man's wisdom teaches but which the Holy Spirit teaches, comparing spiritual things with spiritual. But the natural man does not receive the things of the Spirit of God, for they are foolishness to him; nor can he know them, because they are spiritually discerned. But he who is spiritual judges all things, yet he himself is rightly judged by no one. For "who has known the mind of the LORD that he may instruct Him?" But we have the mind of Christ."

1 Corinthians 4:1–20

"Let a man so consider us, as servants of Christ and stewards of the mysteries of God. Moreover it is required in stewards that one be found faithful. But with me it is a very small thing that I should be judged by you or by a human court. In fact, I do not even judge myself. For I know of nothing against myself, yet I am not justified by this; but He who judges me is the Lord. Therefore judge nothing before the time, until the Lord comes, who will both bring to light the hidden things of darkness and reveal the counsels of the hearts. Then each one's praise will come from God. Now these things, brethren, I have figuratively transferred to myself and Apollos for your sakes, that you may learn in us not to think beyond what is written, that none of you may be puffed up on behalf of one against the other. For who makes you differ from another? And what do you have that you did not receive? Now if you did indeed receive it, why do you boast as if you had not received it? You are already full! You are already rich! You have reigned as kings without us--and indeed I could wish you did reign, that we also might reign with you! For I think that God has displayed us, the apostles, last, as men condemned to death; for we have been made a spectacle to the world, both to angels and to men. We are fools for Christ's sake, but you are wise in Christ! We are weak, but you are strong! You are distinguished, but we are dishonored! To the present hour we both hunger and thirst, and we are poorly clothed, and beaten, and homeless. And we labor, working with our own hands. Being reviled, we bless; being persecuted, we endure; being defamed, we entreat. We have been made as the filth of the world, the offscouring of all things until now. I do not write these things to shame you, but as my beloved children I warn you. For though you might have ten thousand instructors in Christ, yet you do not have many fathers; for in Christ Jesus I have begotten you through the gospel. Therefore I urge you, imitate me. For this reason I have sent Timothy to you, who is my beloved and faithful son in the Lord, who will remind you of my ways in Christ, as I teach everywhere in every church. Now some are puffed up, as though I were not coming to you. But I will come to you shortly, if the Lord wills, and I will know, not the word of those who are puffed up, but the power. For the kingdom of God is not in word but in power."

Quotes

"There is no craving in the human heart more persistent or more passionate than the craving to lay a firm hand upon something eternal. And only the preacher whose eyes are lit by the inner fires of profound conviction can hope to lead those groping pilgrims to their shining goal."

— F.W. Boreham

"The Bible divides all the human race into two classes only; the righteous and the wicked."

— Charles G. Finney

"Go for souls. Go straight for souls, and go for the worst."

— William Booth

"I have but one passion, it is he, it is he alone. The world is the field and the field is the world; and henceforth that country shall be my home where I can be most used in winning soul for Christ."

— Count Zinzindorf

"Tell the young, tell the poor, tell the aged, tell the ignorant, tell the sick, tell the dying—tell them all about Christ. Tell them of His power, and tell them of His love; tell them of His doings, and tell them of His feelings; tell them what He has done for the chief of sinners; tell them what He is willing to do until the last day of time; tell it to them over and over again. Never be tired of speaking of Christ. Say to them broadly and fully, freely and unconditionally, unreservedly and undoubtingly, 'Come unto Christ, as the penitent thief did; come unto Christ, and you shall be saved."

— J.C. Ryle

"In the Kingdom you have what you share."

— Sadhu Sundar Singh

"In the streets a man must from beginning to end be intense, and for that very reason he must be condensed and concentrated in his thought and utterances."

— John Wesley

"I don't preach like I love people, I live like I love people, I love my enemy, like I love my best friend, even my brother who beat me blind knows that I love him."

— Holy Hubert Lindsey

"Before I can preach love, mercy, and grace, I must preach sin, law, and judgment."

— John Wesley

"You are not here in the world for yourself. You have been sent here for others. The world is waiting for you!"

— Catherine Booth

"If Jesus preached the same message ministers preach today, He would have never been crucified."

— Leonard Ravenhill

"I believe I never was more acceptable to my Master than when I was standing to teach those hearers in the open fields I now preach to ten times more people than I would if I had been confined to the churches."

— George Whitefield

"Give me one hundred preachers who fear nothing but sin and desire nothing but God, and I care not whether they be clergymen or laymen, they alone will shake the gates of Hell and set up the kingdom of Heaven upon Earth."

— John Wesley

"No sort of defense is needed for preaching outdoors, but it would take a very strong argument to prove that a man who has never preached beyond the walls of his meetinghouse has done his duty. A defense is required for services within buildings rather than for worship outside of them."

— Charles Haddon Spurgeon

"This generation is responsible for this generation of souls."

— Keith Green

"Oh, that I had a thousand lives and a thousand bodies! All of them should be devoted to no other employment but to preach Christ to these degraded, despised, yet beloved mortals."

— Robert Moffat

"The fearful are caught as often as the bold."

— Helen Keller

"Salt, when dissolved in water, may disappear, but it does not cease to exist. We can be sure of its presence by tasting the water. Likewise, the indwelling Christ, though unseen, will be made evident to others from the love which he imparts to us."

— Sadhu Sundar Singh

"You cannot sacrifice discipleship for evangelism and you cannot sacrifice evangelism for discipleship."

— Curt Harlow

"The man who would win the world for Christ—one of Christ's passionate few—must walk the city streets secretly exulting in the thought of his Savior: he will repeat to himself the name of his Lord as a lover repeats to himself the lovely name of his lady. O Jesus, Jesus, dearest Lord, Forgive me if I say, For very love, Thy precious Name A thousand times a day. Each separate member of the passionate few will find his faith so enjoyable, so delectable, so exciting that the very mention of his Savior's name will awaken all his enthusiasm, stir all his devotion, inflame all the faculties of his soul, and shine out lustrously from his very countenance."

— F.W. Boreham

Maxims

- You already are a witness.
- You might be the only Bible others get the chance to read.
- Just a little bit of courage.
- It's not hard to share good news.
- Truth is seen as hate to those who hate the truth.

Discussion Questions

1) Is it really hard to spread good news?
2) How does the fundamental of discipleship complement the fundamental of evangelism and vice versa?
3) What is the primary objective of evangelism?

Practical Challenges

1) Share your testimony with complete strangers over fifteen separate times. Practice on a friend or small group leader first. Spread the fifteen testimonies out over five weeks. Three times a week establishes regularity in witness.
2) Sharing your personal testimony is the building block of evangelism. (Write it out on paper first).
3) Share the story of Jesus (pure evangelism). Tell the story of Jesus: his birth, life, teachings, commands, and death, burial, and resurrection.
4) Learn and develop the Ezra method of evangelism. It's as simple as taking your Bible, opening it up, and pointing to a verse and asking, "What do you think about this?" The next step is that of public reading of scripture and then answering questions that the newly gathered crowd has asked.

Further Study

Youth Aflame ("Andrew" chapter), Winkie Pratney
A Faith to Proclaim, James S. Stewart
The Wondrous Joy of Soul Winning, R.A. Torrey
How to Work for Christ, R.A. Torrey
The Divine Art of Soul Winning, J. Oswald Sanders
The Normal Christian Birth, David Pawson
The Road to Hell, David Pawson
The Preacher's Portrait, John W. Stott
Bless Your Dirty Heart, Hubert Lindsey
Boulevards of Paradise (The Passionate Few), F.W. Boreham
The General Next to God, Richard Collier
Who Will Rise Up, Jed Smock

Wesley's Veterans, Epworth Press
The Suffering of God, Terence E. Fretheim
How to Preach, William Booth
Personal Work, R.A. Torrey
Autobiography of Charles G. Finney
Born to Reproduce, Dawson Trotman (Sermon)
The Doctrine of Endless Punishment, William Greenough Thayer Shedd

CHAPTER 20: MISSIONS

"The earth is the LORD's, and all its fullness, The world and those who dwell therein." — Psalm 24:1

The nations belong to God by noble right. The rebellion of man and the enslavement by the enemy has blinded and darkened the minds of millions. Christ, the light of the world, has commanded his church to bear the flaming torches of truth and liberty to the souls that sit in darkness. This commandment to go to all nations must once again be sounded as the rallying cry for the mighty army of God. All Christians have their place in the great mission of God and must be faithful soldiers in this last conquest for Christ throughout the earth, to reclaim for him his due reward.

Scriptures

John 20:21

> "So Jesus said to them again, "Peace to you! As the Father has sent Me, I also send you."

Isaiah 6:8

> "Also I heard the voice of the Lord, saying: "Whom shall I send, And who will go for Us?" Then I said, "Here am I! Send me."

Ephesians 3:8

> "To me, who am less than the least of all the saints, this grace was given, that I should preach among the Gentiles the unsearchable riches of Christ."

Luke 19:10

> "For the Son of Man has come to seek and to save that which was lost."

Luke 5:32

>"I have not come to call the righteous, but sinners, to repentance."

Matthew 9:37–38

>"Then He said to His disciples, "The harvest truly is plentiful, but the laborers are few. "Therefore pray the Lord of the harvest to send out laborers into His harvest."

John 12:24–26

>"Most assuredly, I say to you, unless a grain of wheat falls into the ground and dies, it remains alone; but if it dies, it produces much grain. "He who loves his life will lose it, and he who hates his life in this world will keep it for eternal life. "If anyone serves Me, let him follow Me; and where I am, there My servant will be also. If anyone serves Me, him My Father will honor."

Matthew 22:14

>"For many are called, but few are chosen."

Ecclesiastes 3:11

>"He has made everything beautiful in its time. Also He has put eternity in their hearts, except that no one can find out the work that God does from beginning to end."

Acts 26:18

>"To open their eyes, in order to turn them from darkness to light, and from the power of Satan to God, that they may receive forgiveness of sins and an inheritance among those who are sanctified by faith in Me."

Quotes

"While women weep, as they do now, I'll fight; while little children go hungry, I'll fight; while men go to prison, in and out, in and out, as they do now, I'll fight—while there is a drunkard left, while there is a poor lost girl upon the streets, where there remains one dark soul without the light of God—I'll fight! I'll fight to the very end!"

— William Booth

"He was 'the Savior of the world' (John 4:42). God wanted all men to be saved and to come to a knowledge of the truth. To that end Jesus gave himself to provide a salvation from all sin for all men. In that he died for one, he died for all. Contrary to our superficial thinking, there never was a distinction in his mind between home and foreign missions. To Jesus it was all world evangelism."

— Robert E. Coleman

"There are three indispensable requirements for a missionary:
1. Patience, 2. Patience, 3. Patience."

— Hudson Taylor

"Today Christians spend more money on dog food than missions."

— Leonard Ravenhill

"To know the will of God, we need an open Bible and an open map."

— William Carey

"The Great Commission is not an option to be considered; it is a command to be obeyed."

— Hudson Taylor

"Expect great things from God; attempt great things for God."

— William Carey

"He is no fool who gives up what he cannot keep to gain that which he cannot lose."

— Jim Elliot

"If a commission by an earthly king is considered a honor, how can a commission by a Heavenly King be considered a sacrifice?"

— David Livingston

"Missions is an expression of our hope."
— Bishop Lesslie Newbigin

"Missions is church planting amongst the unreached."
— Dick Brogden

"Some wish to live within the sound of a chapel bell; I wish to run a rescue mission within a yard of hell."
— C.T. Studd

"If Jesus Christ be God and died for me, then no sacrifice can be too great for me to make for Him."
— C.T. Studd

"The mission of the church is missions."
— Oswald J. Smith

"Missions begins with a kind of an explosion of joy. The news that the crucified and rejected Jesus is alive it's something that cannot possibly be suppressed. It must be told."
— Bishop Lesslie Newbigin

"We talk of the Second Coming; half the world has never heard of the first."
— Oswald J. Smith

"No reserves. No retreats. No regrets."
— William Borden

"Someone asked, 'Will the heathen who have never heard the Gospel be saved?' It is more a question with me whether we who have the Gospel and fail to give it to those who have not—can be saved."
— Charles Spurgeon

Maxims

- If everyone is a missionary then no one is.
- 42% of the world is unreached, 3.15 billion are lost with limited to no access to the Gospel
- 97% of Christian money goes to Christian places.
- Find, feed, and fight for the lambs of God.
- Every student gives, every student goes, every student prays, every student welcomes.
- Let your eyes affect your heart.
- Love finds a need and meets it.
- If you want a friend, be a friend.
- You're either a missionary or a mission field.

Discussion Questions

1) How many unreached people groups can you name?
2) How do we develop apostolic passion for the lost world?
3) What role does proclamation have in global missions?

Practical Challenges

1) Begin to pray about taking a short-term mission trip.
2) Support a missionary with prayer and finances. (The price of four starbucks drinks a month is substantial support to a missionary.)
3) Use the world news agencies to act as prayer requests for the world. Also download and use the Operation World App as a way to pray specifically for the lost world.
4) Commit to evangelism and service here before you consider work abroad.

Further Study

Eternity in Their Hearts, Don Richardson
The Peace Child, Don Richardson
The Doctrine of Endless Punishment, William Greenough Thayer Shedd
Born to Reproduce, Dawson Trotman (Sermon)

Operation World (7th Edition), Patrick Johnstone
Strongholds of the 10/40 Window, George Otis, Jr.
God's Smuggler, Brother Andrew
The Solitary Throne, Samuel Zwemer
How I Found Livingstone, Henry M. Stanley
Life of St. Patrick, J.B. Bury
L'Abri, Edith Schaeffer
Bruchko, Bruce Olson
The Life and Diary of David Brainerd, Jonathan Edwards
Insanity of God, Nik Ripkin
Insanity of Obedience, Nik Ripkin
Why You Should Go to the Mission Field, Keith Green
God and Missions Today, Arthur T. Pierson
Live Dead Joy, Dick Brogden
The Divine Art of Soul Winning, J. Oswald Sanders
How Lost Are The Heathen, J. Oswald Sanders
Live Dead Journal: 30 Days of Prayer for Unreached Peoples, 30 Days of Challenge, Live Dead Team compilation

CHAPTER 21: AMBASSADORS OF CHRIST

What a noble privilege to be commissioned by the King of Kings into his service and labor. As Christ's delegated representatives, ambassadors bear the message and responsibility to establish Christ's will and mandate in a hostile land. Ambassadors must maintain the deepest commitment and allegiance to their king and his commission. For they bear the responsibility of representing their king to peoples and nations. Christ asks nothing of us that he himself was not also willing to perform. For Jesus was sent and commissioned by the Father, to bear God's message to a lost humanity. Christ, the first ambassador, accomplished his mission and now has perpetuated a movement in which men and women have joined him in his commission.

Scriptures

1 Corinthians 1:17–18

"For Christ did not send me to baptize, but to preach the gospel, not with wisdom of words, lest the cross of Christ should be made of no effect. For the message of the cross is foolishness to those who are perishing, but to us who are being saved it is the power of God."

2 Corinthians 5:11

"Knowing, therefore, the terror of the Lord, we persuade men; but we are well known to God, and I also trust are well known in your consciences."

2 Corinthians 5:18–20

"Now all things are of God, who has reconciled us to Himself through Jesus Christ, and has given us the ministry of reconciliation, that is, that God was in Christ reconciling the world to Himself, not imputing their trespasses to them, and has committed to us the word of reconciliation. Now then, we are ambassadors for Christ, as though God were pleading through us: we implore you on Christ's behalf, be reconciled to God."

John 9:4
"I must work the works of Him who sent Me while it is day; the night is coming when no one can work."

Colossians 1:27–28
"To them God willed to make known what are the riches of the glory of this mystery among the Gentiles: which is Christ in you, the hope of glory. Him we preach, warning every man and teaching every man in all wisdom, that we may present every man perfect in Christ Jesus."

2 Timothy 2:2
"And the things that you have heard from me among many witnesses, commit these to faithful men who will be able to teach others also."

Quotes

"Only one life, 'twill soon be past, only what's done for Christ will last. And when I am dying, how happy I'll be, if the lamp of my life has been burned out for Thee."

— C.T. Studd

"We are not diplomats but prophets, and our message is not a compromise but an ultimatum."

— A.W. Tozer

"Lord, stamp eternity on my eyeballs."

— Jonathan Edwards

"The man in Christ Jesus is no longer self-centered, but God-centered."

— G. Campbell Morgan

"I care not where I go, or how I live, or what I endure so that I may save souls. When I sleep I dream of them; when I awake they are first in my thoughts."

— David Brainerd

"Could a mariner sit idle if he heard the drowning cry? Could a doctor sit in comfort and just let his patients die? Could a fireman sit idle, let men burn and give no hand? Can you sit at ease in Zion with the world around you *damned*?"

— Leonard Ravenhill

"Make it an object of constant study, and of daily reflection and prayer, to learn how to deal with sinners so as to promote their conversion."

— Charles G. Finney

"There are four facts concerning Christ which cannot be disputed by any person of intelligence and honesty...Let me state them in order. Christ is the revealer of the highest type of human life. Christ is the redeemer of all types of human failure. Christ is the ruler over the most remarkable empire that man has ever seen. Christ is demonstrated the restorer of lost order, wherever He is obeyed."

— G. Campbell Morgan

"I'd rather have people hate me with the knowledge that I tried to save them."

— Keith Green

"There is no joy in the world like the joy of bringing one soul to Christ."

— William Barclay

"Love your fellowmen, and cry about them if you cannot bring them to Christ. If you cannot save them, you can weep over them. If you cannot give them a drop of cold water in hell, you can give them your heart's tears while they are still in this body."

— Charles Spurgeon

"Do all the good you can by all the means you can in all the places you can at all the times you can to all the people you can as long as ever you can."

— John Wesley

"Hast thou no scar?
No hidden scar on foot, or side, or hand?
I hear thee sung as mighty in the land,
I hear them hail thy bright ascendant star,
Hast thou no scar?
Hast thou no wound?
Yet I was wounded by the archers, spent,
Leaned Me against a tree to die, and rent
by ravening beasts that compassed Me, I swooned:
Hast thou no wound?
No wound, no scar?
Yet as the Master shall the servant be,
And, pierced are the feet that follow Me;
But thine are whole: can he have followed far
Who has no wound nor scar?"

— Amy Carmichael

Vows of Spiritual Power by: A.W. Tozer

These concepts and convictions were instrumental in transforming my character. I use them as a constant guidepost and encouragement to a deeper life in Christ. They have been a refinement and a safeguard to me and countless others. These convictions will truly help form and preserve the heart of an ambassador.

1.) Deal thoroughly with sin in your life and in others.
2.) Never accept any glory.
3.) Never own anything.
4.) Never slander another.
5.) Never defend yourself.

Maxims

- What God does in you, he wants to do through you.
- Discipleship is taking responsibility for what's close to the heart of God.
- Disciples are handcrafted, not mass-produced.
- One person with God is always the majority.
- Your mission field is where your feet are.

Discussion Questions

1) What are the qualities of individuals who represent the kingdom of God?
2) What is the central message of an ambassador?
3) Why are Tozer's five vows of spiritual power, helpful for the maturity of an ambassador?

Practical Challenges

1) Share your testimony with a stranger every day for a week.
2) Ask ten separate people throughout the week if they need prayer.
3) Develop a conviction to enhance a culture of honor.

Further Study

The Company of the Committed, Elton Trueblood
The Lost Art of Discipleship, Leroy Eims
Youth Aflame, Winkie Pratney
The Master Plan of Evangelism, Robert E. Coleman
The Master Plan of Discipleship, Robert E. Coleman
Spiritual Leadership, J. Oswald Sanders
Spiritual Lesson, J. Oswald Sanders
Spiritual Maturity, J. Oswald Sanders
A Spiritual Clinic, J. Oswald Sanders
Fishers of Men, William Barclay
Preacher's Portrait, John W. Stott

The General Next to God, Richard Collier
So Send I You, Oswald Chambers
Wesley's Veterans, Epworth Publishing
The Seven Spirits, General William Booth
So Great a Salvation, Charles G. Finney
The Suffering of God, Terence E. Fretheim

CHAPTER 22: SPIRITUAL DISCIPLINES

Discipline is the essential and indispensable component to the Christian life. Every man who is used of God is a disciplined man. We know this to be true regardless of the field of study or occupation. The root word of "disciple" is that of discipline. One cannot be a disciple of Christ without consistently refining themselves in the Lord's disciplines. Many countless people wait for God to move in their life, while the Spirit waits patiently to flow through the hewn channels of discipline.

Scriptures

The following points are compiled from the works of Richard Foster's *Celebration of Discipline.*

Inward Disciplines

The inner life and devotion of a Christian cannot be seen directly but will always reveal itself in times of trial and temptation. The fruit of the Spirit will grow abundantly in the heart of a disciplined mind.

Meditation

Psalm 1:1–3

> "Blessed is the man Who walks not in the counsel of the ungodly, Nor stands in the path of sinners, Nor sits in the seat of the scornful; But his delight is in the law of the LORD, And in His law he meditates day and night. He shall be like a tree Planted by the rivers of water, That brings forth its fruit in its season, Whose leaf also shall not wither; And whatever he does shall prosper."

Prayer

James 5:16

> "Confess your trespasses to one another, and pray for one another, that you may be healed. The effective, fervent prayer of a righteous man avails much."

Fasting

Matthew 6:17–18

> "But you, when you fast, anoint your head and wash your face, "so that you do not appear to men to be fasting, but to your Father who is in the secret place; and your Father who sees in secret will reward you openly."

Study

John 8:32

> "And you shall know the truth, and the truth shall make you free."

Outward Disciplines

With the inward disciplines rooted and established in love, the outward disciplines come to flourish and blossom, revealing the fragrance of Christ.

Simplicity

Proverbs 11:28

> "He who trusts in his riches will fall, But the righteous will flourish like foliage."

Solitude

Matthew 14:23–24

> "And when He had sent the multitudes away, He went up on the mountain by Himself to pray. Now when evening came, He was alone there. But the boat was now in the middle of the sea, tossed by the waves, for the wind was contrary."

Submission

Ephesians 5:21
> "Submitting to one another in the fear of God."

Service

Galatians 5:13
> "For you, brethren, have been called to liberty; only do not use liberty as an opportunity for the flesh, but through love serve one another."

Corporate Disciplines

The purpose of the inward and outward disciplined life is to demonstrate its love for both God and man. The greatest commandment Christ ever gave was to love God, and the second was like it—to love our neighbor as ourselves. To love Christ is also to love his body, the church. A wise man will understand his great need for God and his great need for others. The Gospel flows through community and our relationships.

Confession

James 5:16
> "*Confess your trespasses to one another, and pray for one another, that you may be healed.* The effective, fervent prayer of a righteous man avails much." (Emphasis added)

Worship

John 4:23
> "But the hour is coming, and now is, when the true worshipers will worship the Father in spirit and truth; for the Father is seeking such to worship Him."

Guidance

Proverbs 3:5–6
> "Trust in the LORD with all your heart, And lean not on your

own understanding; In all your ways acknowledge Him, And
He shall direct your paths."

Celebration

John 15:11

"These things I have spoken to you, that My joy may remain
in you, and that your joy may be full."

Quotes

"Nothing can be more hurtful to the service, than the neglect of
discipline; for that discipline, more than numbers, gives one army the
superiority over another."

— George Washington

"We cannot bear the same kind of fruit unless we are the same kind of
tree. So He wants to make us like Himself."

— Samuel Logan Brengle

"All the great temptations appear first in the region of the mind and
can be fought and conquered there. We have been given the power to
close the door of the mind. We can lose this power through disuse or
increase it by use, by the daily discipline of the inner man in things
which seem small and by reliance upon the word of the Spirit of truth.
It is God that worketh in you, both to will and to do of His
good pleasure. It is as though He said, 'Learn to live in your will, not
in your feelings.'"

— Amy Carmichael

"The sweetest scents are only obtained by tremendous pressure; the
fairest flowers grow amid Alpine snow-solitudes; the fairest gems
have suffered longest from the lapidary's wheel; the noblest statues
have borne most blows of the chisel. All, however, are under law.
Nothing happens that has not been appointed with consummate care
and foresight."

— F.B. Meyer

"Those who determine not to put self to death will never see the will of God fulfilled in their lives. Those who ought to become the light of the world must necessarily burn and become less and less. By denying self, we are able to win others."

— Sadhu Sundar Singh

"The battle of prayer is against two things in the earthlies: wandering thoughts and lack of intimacy with God's character as revealed in His word. Neither can be cured at once, but they can be cured by discipline."

— Oswald Chambers

"Service is a badge of royalty and a distinguishing mark of the sons of God and citizens of heavenly upon earth."

— Samuel Logan Brengle

"A farmer is helpless to grow grain; all he can do is provide the right conditions for the growing of grain. He cultivates the ground, he plants the seed, he waters the plants, and then the natural forces of the earth take over and up comes the grain...This is the way it is with the Spiritual Disciplines—they are a way of sowing to the Spirit...By themselves the Spiritual Disciplines can do nothing; they can only get us to the place where something can be done."

— Richard J. Foster

"Discipline brings freedom."

— Richard J. Foster

His Plan for Me
"When I stand at the Judgment Seat of Christ
And He shows His plan for me,
The plan of my life as it might have been
Had He had His way - and I see
How I blocked Him here, and checked Him there,
And I would not yield my will,
Will there be grief in my Savior's eyes,
Grief though He loves me still?

Would He have me rich and I stand there poor,
Stripped of all but His grace,
While memory runs like a hunted thing,
Down the paths I cannot retrace.
Lord, of the years that are left to me
I give them to Thy hand
Take me and break me and mold me,
To the pattern that Thou hast planned!"

— Author Unknown

Maxims

- Leaders are readers.
- A disciple is disciplined.
- Every man of God is a disciplined man.
- The word "disciple" comes from "discipline."
- Discipline brings freedom.
- The cost of making a disciple is being one.

Discussion Questions

1) How do the outward and corporate disciplines flow from the inward ones?
2) How did Jesus model the discipline of prayer in his earthly ministry?
3) How does discipline bring freedom?

Practical Challenges

1) Pray and discipline your weakest area in spiritual disciplines.
2) Spend an entire day alone with God in solitude.
3) Fast for one day.
4) Give something away, (the only qualification is that it hurts to do so).

Further Study

Christian Disciplines, Vol. 1 & 2, Oswald Chambers
Celebration of Discipline, Richard J. Foster
Victorious Christian Service, Alan Redpath
The Imitation of Christ, Thomas à Kempis
The Royal Way of the Cross, Francois Fenelon
Why Revival Tarries, Leonard Ravenhill
The Fellowship of the Saints, Thomas S. Kepler
In the Footprints of the Lamb, G. Steinberger
David Brainerd, His Message for Today, Oswald J. Smith
Spiritual Classics, Richard J. Foster and Emilie Griffin
Devotional Classics, Richard J. Foster and James Bryan Smith
The Spirit of the Disciplines, Dallas Willard
Disciplined Life, Richard Taylor
Meat for Men, Leonard Ravenhill

CHAPTER 23: GUIDANCE

The great calling of a Christian is to be led by the Spirit of God. The highest privilege is to hear his voice and to recognize his impressions on our conscience and heart. The promises of the scriptures speak of continual guidance, light, and revelation in his path. One must use wisdom and caution in discerning the will of God. *"Enter by the narrow gate; for wide is the gate and broad is the way that leads to destruction, and there are many who go in by it,"* (Matthew 7:13). But the meek he will guide in judgment.

Scriptures

Romans 8:14

"For as many as are led by the Spirit of God, these are sons of God."

Acts 8:26–27

"Now an angel of the Lord spoke to Philip, saying, "Arise and go toward the south along the road which goes down from Jerusalem to Gaza." This is desert. So he arose and went. And behold, a man of Ethiopia, a eunuch of great authority under Candace the queen of the Ethiopians, who had charge of all her treasury, and had come to Jerusalem to worship.""

Galatians 1:11–12

"But I make known to you, brethren, that the gospel which was preached by me is not according to man. For I neither received it from man, nor was I taught it, but it came through the revelation of Jesus Christ."

Isaiah 58:11

"The LORD will guide you continually, And satisfy your soul in drought, And strengthen your bones; You shall be like a watered garden, And like a spring of water, whose waters do not fail."

John 8:12

> "Then Jesus spoke to them again, saying, "I am the light of the world. He who follows Me shall not walk in darkness, but have the light of life.""

1 Thessalonians 5:21

> "Test all things; hold fast what is good."

Acts 17:11–12

> "These were more fair-minded than those in Thessalonica, in that they received the word with all readiness, and searched the Scriptures daily to find out whether these things were so. Therefore many of them believed, and also not a few of the Greeks, prominent women as well as men."

Luke 11:34

> "The lamp of the body is the eye. Therefore, when your eye is good, your whole body also is full of light. But when your eye is bad, your body also is full of darkness."

John 5:30

> "I can of Myself do nothing. As I hear, I judge; and My judgment is righteous, because I do not seek My own will but the will of the Father who sent Me."

1 John 4:1–4

> "Beloved, do not believe every spirit, but test the spirits, whether they are of God; because many false prophets have gone out into the world. By this you know the Spirit of God: Every spirit that confesses that Jesus Christ has come in the flesh is of God, and every spirit that does not confess that Jesus Christ has come in the flesh is not of God. And this is the spirit of the Antichrist, which you have heard was coming, and is now already in the world. You are of God, little children, and have overcome them, because He who is in you is greater than he who is in the world."

Proverbs 3:5–6

> "Trust in the LORD with all your heart, And lean not on your own understanding; In all your ways acknowledge Him, And He shall direct your paths."

Proverbs 15:22

> "Without counsel, plans go awry, But in the multitude of counselors they are established."

Wisdom Concerning Guidance

The Peace of God

A great guidepost in discerning guidance from God is, do you have the peace of God on your decision. The wisdom from Paul's epistle to the Colossians says to "let the peace of God rule in your hearts, to which also you were called in one body; and be thankful," (Colossians 3:15).

Affirmation from Godly Brother and Sisters

"What do you think about this?" is one of the wisest questions one can ask in seeking counsel for our lives. The Proverbs say, "that a man who isolates himself seeks his own desires."

Confirmation by Divine Providence

Supernatural events, corresponding with the leading of the Spirit, act as encouraging confirmation. This is not, however, random occurrences, or observer bias, but rather supernatural confirmation.

The Word of God is still the lamp and light

We must not diminish the authority and power of the Bible to give insight and direction to a saint's life. "Your word is a lamp to my feet And a light to my path." Psalms 119:105

Quotes

"God's impressions within and His word without are always coordinated by His providence around, and we should quietly wait until these three focus into one point."

— F.B. Meyer

"Start by doing what's necessary; then do what's possible; and suddenly you are doing the impossible."

— Francis of Assisi

"Men give advice; God gives guidance."

— Leonard Ravenhill

"When God speaks He speaks so loudly that all the voices of the world seem dumb. And yet when God speaks He speaks so softly that no one hears the whisper but yourself."

— Henry Drummond

"Mind the light of God in your consciences, which will show you all deceit; dwelling in it, guides out of the many things into one spirit, which cannot lie, nor deceive. Those who are guided by it are one."

— George Fox

"Obviously God must guide us in a way that will develop spontaneity in us. The development of character, rather than direction in this, that, and the other matter, must be the primary purpose of the Father. He will guide us, but he won't override us. That fact should make us use with caution the method of sitting down with a pencil and blank sheet of paper to write down the instructions dictated by God for the day. Suppose a parent would dictate to the child minutely everything he is to do during the day. The child would be stunted under that regime. The parent must guide in such a manner, and to the degree, that autonomous character, capable of making right decisions for itself, is produced. God does the same."

— E. Stanley Jones

"Let us look high enough for guidance. Let us encourage our soul to wait only upon God till it is given. Let us cultivate that meekness which He will guide in judgment. Let us seek to be of quick understanding, that we may be apt to see the least sign of His will. Let us stand with girded loins and lighted lamps that we may be prompt to obey. Blessed are those servants. They shall be led by a right way to the golden city of the saints."

— F.B. Meyer

Maxims

- Feelings follow right action.
- Meekness is not weakness.
- Our motives must be pure and our will surrendered.
- There is wisdom in a multitude of council.
- The Holy Spirit will never contradict the word of God.

Discussion Questions

1) How do we distinguish what the voice of God is? What are the trademarks of his voice?
2) What do we do if the revelation and impression we are receiving is in conflict with the teachings of the word of God?
3) There's wisdom in a multitude of council. How do we apply this in life decisions?
4) What is the definition of meekness?

Practical Challenges

1) Pray that God would reveal areas in your life where you could be a better servant.
2) Pray for guidance for others.

Further Study

Youth Aflame ("Phillip" Chapter), Winkie Pratney
God's Trademarks, George Otis, Jr.

Chapter 23: Guidance

The Secret of Guidance, F.B. Meyer
Hearing God, Dallas Willard
Knowing God's Will, (Article), Winkie Pratney
Answers to Prayer, George Müller
The Cross and the Switchblade, David Wilkerson
Humility, Andrew Murray
Ultimate Core, (Conditions of Guidance Section), Winkie Pratney
Spiritual Lessons, J. Oswald Sanders
Deeper Christian Life, Andrew Murray
George Müller of Bristol, A.T. Pierson
Insanity of God, Nik Ripkin

CHAPTER 24: LIFE IN THE SPIRIT

From the pages of Acts to the plains of Africa, miraculous signs have followed those who believe. The God of the Bible is a God of miracles. These wondrous demonstrations of his power should not be an end in and of themselves but rather a compliment to his character. God is at work through his people, and the acts of the Holy Spirit have not ended. For the promises of the prophet ring true today, *"Those who do wickedly against the covenant he shall corrupt with flattery; but the people who know their God shall be strong, and carry out great exploits."* (Daniel 11:32). However, as great and majestic as these spiritual manifestations of power can be, the genuine fruit and character of the Spirit exemplified consistently and holistically in the life of every follower is still the ideal.

Scriptures

1 Corinthians 1:7

> "So that you come short in no gift, eagerly waiting for the revelation of our Lord Jesus Christ."

Galatians 5:22–26

> "But the fruit of the Spirit is love, joy, peace, longsuffering, kindness, goodness, faithfulness, gentleness, self-control. Against such there is no law. And those who are Christ's have crucified the flesh with its passions and desires. If we live in the Spirit, let us also walk in the Spirit. Let us not become conceited, provoking one another, envying one another."

1 Corinthians 12:1–11

> "Now concerning spiritual gifts, brethren, I do not want you to be ignorant: You know that you were Gentiles, carried away to these dumb idols, however you were led. Therefore I make known to you that no one speaking by the Spirit of God calls Jesus accursed, and no one can say that Jesus is Lord except by the Holy Spirit. There are diversities of gifts, but the same Spirit. There are differences of ministries, but the same Lord.

And there are diversities of activities, but it is the same God who works all in all. But the manifestation of the Spirit is given to each one for the profit of all: for to one is given the word of wisdom through the Spirit, to another the word of knowledge through the same Spirit, to another faith by the same Spirit, to another gifts of healings by the same Spirit, to another the working of miracles, to another prophecy, to another discerning of spirits, to another different kinds of tongues, to another the interpretation of tongues. But one and the same Spirit works all these things, distributing to each one individually as He wills."

2 Corinthians 3:17–18

"Now the Lord is the Spirit; and where the Spirit of the Lord is, there is liberty. But we all, with unveiled face, beholding as in a mirror the glory of the Lord, are being transformed into the same image from glory to glory, just as by the Spirit of the Lord."

John 3:5–8

"Jesus answered, "Most assuredly, I say to you, unless one is born of water and the Spirit, he cannot enter the kingdom of God. "That which is born of the flesh is flesh, and that which is born of the Spirit is spirit. "Do not marvel that I said to you, 'You must be born again.' "The wind blows where it wishes, and you hear the sound of it, but cannot tell where it comes from and where it goes. So is everyone who is born of the Spirit."

Genesis 1:2

"The earth was without form, and void; and darkness was on the face of the deep. And the Spirit of God was hovering over the face of the waters."

John 16:13–16

"However, when He, the Spirit of truth, has come, He will guide you into all truth; for He will not speak on His own authority, but whatever He hears He will speak; and He will tell you things to come. "He will glorify Me, for He will take of what is Mine and declare it to you. "All things that the Father has are Mine. Therefore I said that He will take of Mine and declare it to you. "A little while, and you will not see Me; and again a little while, and you will see Me, because I go to the Father."

2 Timothy 1:6–7

"Therefore I remind you to stir up the gift of God which is in you through the laying on of my hands. For God has not given us a spirit of fear, but of power and of love and of a sound mind."

1 Thessalonians 5:19

"Do not quench the Spirit."

Joel 2:28

"And it shall come to pass afterward That I will pour out My Spirit on all flesh; Your sons and your daughters shall prophesy, Your old men shall dream dreams, Your young men shall see visions."

Romans 12:6–8

"Having then gifts differing according to the grace that is given to us, let us use them: if prophecy, let us prophesy in proportion to our faith; or ministry, let us use it in our ministering; he who teaches, in teaching; he who exhorts, in exhortation; he who gives, with liberality; he who leads, with diligence; he who shows mercy, with cheerfulness."

Gifts Explained

Three to Speak

Prophecy: Prophecy is declaring the mind of God with conviction, power, and clarity. Prophecy is not primarily prediction of the unforeseen, but rather, Spirit-inspired confrontation, which results in conviction and repentance (1 Corinthians 12:7–11, Acts 13:1, Acts 15:32, Acts 21:10).

Various Kinds of Tongues: Praying in the spirit is an ecstatic utterance for corporate edification. This unlearned, unknown language, although it is described as the least of the gifts, has been a distinctive charisma of the people of the Spirit, empowering and encouraging them since Pentecost (1 Corinthians 12:7–11, 1 Corinthians 14, Acts 2).

Interpretation of Various Kinds of Tongues: An interpretation of tongues is clearly mandated from the wisdom of Paul's pastorate. This divinely given interpretation is for corporate edification and should always be coupled with the corporate gift of tongues (1 Corinthians 12:7–11, Acts 2, 1 Corinthians 14).

Three to Know

Word of Wisdom: A word of wisdom is a supernatural provision of divine wisdom that brings guidance and direction to the body of Christ (1 Corinthians 12:7–11, Acts 6:10).

Word of Knowledge: A word of knowledge is a supernatural understanding and comprehension of facts or information that was given solely by God. This is not derived from normal faculties but is revealed to the mind through the Spirit (1 Corinthians 12:7–11).

Discernment of Spirits: Discernment in this regard has to do with a divine revelation of spiritual forces at work and whether such influences are from God or from demonic sources. This is more than just having discernment that comes from Biblical maturity, but rather, a specialized ability given by the Holy Spirit (1 Corinthians 12:7–11, Acts 16:16–24, 2 Kings 5:26).

Three to Act

Healing: A gift of healing is the miraculous removal of illness and diseases from the individual body. The gift of healing can also be that of emotional and spiritual healing from many worries, cares, or wounds (1 Corinthians 12:7–11, James 5:14–15, Psalm 103:3, Acts 14:19–28).

Faith: This faith is different than the faith of salvation. Rather, it is an unwavering trust and absolute reliance in Jesus to accomplish a request. It includes visualizing what God wants to accomplish. Examples of this faith would be that of casting out devils, trusting in impossible outcomes, enduring incredible hardships, and martyrdom (1 Corinthians 12:7–11, Acts 6:5).

The Working of Miracles: This involves deeds accomplished through the power of the Spirit. These works usually accompany apostolic proclamation where miraculous events lead to mass conversions, or powerful demonstrations of the character of God (1 Corinthians 12:7–11, Acts 8:7, Acts 19:11).

The Purpose of Spiritual Gifts

The manifestation of the Spirit is for the common good, to equip believers for the service of the church. The ultimate purpose of spiritual gifts is to glorify God through the Spirit.

Psalm 77:13–14
> "Your way, O God, is in the sanctuary; Who is so great a God as our God? You are the God who does wonders; You have declared Your strength among the peoples."

Edify the Body of Christ

1 Corinthians 12:7
> "But the manifestation of the Spirit is given to each one for the profit of all."

1 Corinthians 14:26
> "How is it then, brethren? Whenever you come together, each of you has a psalm, has a teaching, has a tongue, has a

revelation, has an interpretation. Let all things be done for edification."

Demonstrate the Power of God to Validate the Claims of the Gospel

1 Corinthians 2:4

"And my speech and my preaching were not with persuasive words of human wisdom, but in demonstration of the Spirit and of power."

Mark 16:15–20

"And He said to them, "Go into all the world and preach the gospel to every creature. "He who believes and is baptized will be saved; but he who does not believe will be condemned. "And these signs will follow those who believe: In My name they will cast out demons; they will speak with new tongues; "they will take up serpents; and if they drink anything deadly, it will by no means hurt them; they will lay hands on the sick, and they will recover." So then, after the Lord had spoken to them, He was received up into heaven, and sat down at the right hand of God. And they went out and preached everywhere, the Lord working with them and confirming the word through the accompanying signs. Amen."

Hebrews 2:3–4

"How shall we escape if we neglect so great a salvation, which at the first began to be spoken by the Lord, and was confirmed to us by those who heard Him, God also bearing witness both with signs and wonders, with various miracles, and gifts of the Holy Spirit, according to His own will?"

Cautions Concerning these Gifts

One must remember that these are not natural abilities of human capability, but rather divine inspiration for the purpose of corporate edification. These are not uncontrollable experiences that place the believer in a robotic trance-like state, but these gifts are totally subjected to the individual's control. They are also not indicators of Christian maturity and so therefore cannot be badges of honor or markers of growth.

One also must not neglect them, even if others are abusing them, as Paul aptly stated in his Corinthian letter: "So that you come short in no gift, eagerly waiting for the revelation of our Lord Jesus Christ" (1 Corinthians 1:7) and, "Now concerning spiritual *gifts,* brethren, I do not want you to be ignorant:" (1 Corinthians 12:1).

Fruit of the Spirit

Ephesians 5:9
> "For the fruit of the Spirit is in all goodness, righteousness, and truth."

Galatians 5:22–26
> "But the fruit of the Spirit is love, joy, peace, longsuffering, kindness, goodness, faithfulness, gentleness, self-control. Against such there is no law. And those who are Christ's have crucified the flesh with its passions and desires. If we live in the Spirit, let us also walk in the Spirit. Let us not become conceited, provoking one another, envying one another."

Three in Experience

Love: Luke 6:32, 1 John 4:18, 1 John 4:16

Joy: John 15:11, Romans 15:13, Romans 14:16

Peace: Psalm 29:11, Isaiah 26:3, Philippians 4:6–7

"The first of these three triads includes love, joy, and peace, and it is not putting too great a strain on the words to point out that the source of all three lies in the Christian relation to God. They regard nothing but God and our relation to Him; they would be all the same if there were no other men in the world, or if there were no world. We cannot call them duties or virtues; they are simply the results of communion with God—the certain manifestations of the better life of the Spirit. Love, of course, heads the list, as the foundation and moving principle of all the rest. It is the instinctive act of the higher life and is shed abroad in the heart by the Holy Spirit. It is the life sap, which rises through the tree and given form to all the clusters. The remaining two members of this triad are plainly consequences of the first. Joy is not so much an act or a grace of character as an emotion poured into men's lives, because in their hearts abides love to God. Jesus Christ pledged Himself to impart His joy to remain in us, with the issue that our joy should be full. There is only one source of permanent joy which takes possession of and fills all the corners and crannies of the heart, and that is a love towards God equally abiding and all pervasive. We have all known joys so perturbed, fragmentary and fleeting, that it is hard to distinguish them from sorrows, but there is no need that joys should be like green fruits hard and savourless and ready to drop from the tree. If God is 'the gladness of our joy,' and all our delights come from communion with Him, our joy will never pass and will fill the whole round of our spirits as the sea laves every shore. Peace will be built upon love and joy, if our hearts are ever turning to God and ever blessed with the inter-communion of love between Him and us. What can be strong enough to disturb the tranquility that fills the soul independent of all externals? However long and close may be the siege, the well in the castle courtyard will be full. True peace comes not from the absence of trouble but from the presence of God, and will be deep and passing all understanding in the exact measure in which we live in, and partake of, the love of God."

— Alexander MacLaren

Three in Conduct

Patience: 1 Timothy 1:16, Hebrews 6:15, Ephesians 4:2, Romans 12:12

Kindness: Colossians 3:12, 2 Corinthians 6:6, Ephesians 2:7

Goodness: Romans 15:14, Ephesians 5:9, 2 Thessalonians 1:11

"The second triad is long-suffering, kindness, goodness. All these three obviously refer to the spiritual life in its manifestations to men. The first of them—long-suffering—describes the attitude of patient endurance towards inflictors of injury or enemies, if we come forth from the blessed fellowship with God, where love, joy, and peace reign unbroken, and are met with a cold gust of indifference or with an icy wind of hate. The reality of our happy communion and the depth of our love will be tested by the patience of our long-suffering. Love suffereth long, is not easily provoked, is not soon angry. He has little reason to suppose that the love of God is shed abroad in his heart, or that the Spirit of God is bringing forth fruit in him, who has not got beyond the stage of repaying hate with hate, and scorn with scorn. Any fool can answer a fool according to his folly, but it takes a wise and a good man to overcome evil with good, and to love them that hate; and yet how certainly the fires of mutual antagonism would go out if there were only one to pile on the fuel! It takes two to make a quarrel, and no man living under the influence of the Spirit of God can be one of such a pair. The second and third members of this triad—kindness, goodness, slide very naturally into one another. They do not only require the negative virtue of not retaliating, but express the Christian attitude towards all of meeting them, whatever their attitude, with good. It is possible that kindness here expresses the inward disposition and goodness, the habitual actions in which that disposition shows itself. If that be the distinction between them, the former would answer to benevolence and the latter to beneficence. These three graces include all that Paul presents as Christian duty to our fellows. The results of the life of the Spirit are to pass beyond ourselves and to influence our whole conduct. We are not to live only as mainly for the spiritual enjoyments of fellowship with God. The true field of religion is in moving amongst men, and the true basis of all service of men is love and fellowship with God."

— Alexander MacLaren

Three in Character

Faithfulness: 2 Timothy 2:22, Matthew 23:23, 1 John 1:3

Meekness: Colossians 3:12, 2 Corinthians 10:1, Galatians 6:1,
2 Timothy 2:25

Self-control: 2 Peter 1:6, Acts 24:25, 1 Corinthians 9:25

"The third triad—faithfulness, meekness, temperance—seems to point
to the world in which the Christian life is to be lived as a scene of
difficulties and oppositions. The rendering of the Revised Version is
to be preferred to that of the authorized in the first of the three, for it
is not faith in its theological sense to which the Apostle is here
referring. Possibly, however, the meaning may be trustfulness just as
in 1 Corinthians xiii. it is given as a characteristic of love that it
'believeth all things.' More probably, however, the meaning is
faithfulness, and Paul's thought is that the Christian life is to manifest
itself in the faithful discharge of all duties and the honest handling of
all things committed to it. Meekness even more distinctly
contemplates a condition of things, which is contrary to the Christian
life, and points to submissiveness of spirit, which does not lift itself
up against oppositions, but bends like a reed before the storm. Paul
preached meekness and practiced it, but Paul could flash into strong
opposition and with a resonant ring in his voice could say, "To whom
we gave place by subjection, No! not for an hour." The last member
of the triad—temperance—points to the difficulties which the
spiritual life is apt to meet with in the natural passions and desires,
and insists upon the fact that conflict and rigid and habitual self-
control are sure to be marks of that life."

— Alexander MacLaren

Quotes

Fruit of the Spirit

"The gloom of the world is but a shadow; behind it, yet within our
reach, is joy. Take joy."

— Girolamo Savonarola

"In fact, trying to replicate spiritual fruit in your own strength always leads to dead works, whereas abiding in Christ always leads to fruit that has the seed of perpetuating life within it and reproduces itself again and again."

— Jason Bell

"Love is the fruitful mother of bright children. 'A multitude of babes around her hung, playing their sport that joyed her to behold.' Her sons are Strength, and Justice, and Self-control, and Firmness, and Courage, and Patience, and many more besides; and her daughters are Pity with her sad eyes, and Gentleness with her silvery voice, and Mercy whose sweet face makes sunshine in the shade of death, and Humility all unconscious of her loveliness; and linked hand in hand with these, all the radiant band of sisters that men call Virtues and Graces. These will dwell in our hearts, if Love, their mighty mother, be there. If we are without her we shall be without them."

— Alexander Maclaren

"Old leaves, if they remain upon the trees through the autumn and the winter, fall off in the spring." We have seen a hedge all-thick with dry leaves throughout the winter, and neither frost nor wind has removed the withered foliage, but the spring has soon made a clearance. The new life dislodges the old, pushing it away as unsuitable to it. So our old corruptions are best removed by the growth of new graces. 'Old things are passed away; behold, all things are become new.' It is as the new life buds and opens that the old worn-out things of our former state are compelled to quit their hold of us. Our wisdom lies in living near to God, that by the power of His Holy Spirit all our graces may be vigorous, and may exercise a sin-expelling power over our lives: the new leaves of grace pushing off our old sere affections and habits of sin."

— C.H. Spurgeon

"True Christian character is the fruit of the indwelling Spirit."

— J. Oswald Smith

"Peace is greater than all other treasures, but no philosophy can bestow it; for how can philosophy cleanse from sin? Nor can works; for how are they able to justify, descend into whatever mine, shake whatever tree, knock at whatever door in the world thou wilt, the poor world cannot offer it thee. Peace is but one: One only has peace; one only can give it—'the Prince of Peace.'"

— F.W. Krummacher

Spiritual Gifts

"We feel the breath of the wind upon our cheeks, we see the dust and the leaves blowing before the wind, we see the vessels at sea driven swiftly towards their ports; but the wind itself remains invisible. Just so with the Spirit, we feel His breath upon our souls, we see the mighty things He does, but Himself we do not see. He is invisible, but He is real and perceptible."

— R.A. Torrey

"Love will never edify itself at the expense of stumbling others."

— Donald Gee

"Come, and see the victories of the cross. Christ's wounds are thy healings, His agonies thy repose, His conflicts thy conquests, His groans thy songs, His pains thine ease, His shame thy glory, His death thy life, His sufferings thy salvation."

— Matthew Henry

"Some seek the gifts of the Holy Spirit with genuine earnestness. Yet often what they crave is but some joy, for the 'I' is hidden behind their quest."

— Watchman Nee

"The chief means for attaining wisdom, and suitable gifts for the ministry, are the Holy Scriptures, and prayer."

— John Newton

"Fish which always live in the depths of the ocean lose some of their faculties, like the Tibetan hermits who always live in the dark. The ostrich loses his power of flying because he does not use his wings. Therefore do not bury the gifts and talents which have been given to you, but use them, that you may enter into the joy of your Lord."

— Sadhu Sundar Singh

Maxims

- Be a thermostat, not a thermometer.
- You're as close to God as you want to be.
- The Holy Spirit is often depicted as a dove. The Middle Eastern dove has nine feathers on each wing; there are nine manifestations of spiritual fruit and nine spiritual gifts.
- Seek his heart, not his hand.
- We don't own the gifts. They belong to the Lord.
- Seek the giver, not the gift.

Discussion Questions

1) Does a believer have all the spiritual gifts and how do you know the answer from the scriptures?
2) Can you lack patience and have the fruit of the Spirit?
3) What is the definition of meekness?

Practical Challenges

1) Earnestly desire spiritual gifts; pray and have faith.
2) Ask a mentor/leader if they see the fruit of the Spirit in your life.

Further Study

The Holy Spirit, R.A. Torrey
Surprised by the Power of the Spirit, Jack Deere
Sadhu Sundar Singh, Cyril Davey
The Release of the Spirit, Watchman Nee
The Acts of the Apostles, G. Campbell Morgan

Chapter 24: Life in the Spirit

Concerning Spiritual Gifts, Donald Gee
Fruit of the Spirit, Donald Gee
The Fruit of the Spirit, (Article), SHSU Chi Alpha
Aglow with the Spirit, Dr. Robert Frost
When the Spirit Speaks, Warren Bullock
Divine Order, Randy Hurst
The Spirit Himself, R.M. Riggs
The Complete Collections of His Life and Teachings, John G. Lake
Living in the Spirit, George O. Wood
The Holy Spirit and His Gifts, J. Oswald Sanders
Systematic Theology, Ernest S. Williams
They Speak with Other Tongues, John L. Sherrill
Deeper Experiences of Famous Christians, James G. Lawson

CHAPTER 25: COMMUNION — THE REMEMBRANCE

On the night of the last supper, Jesus instituted a new covenant between God and man, a covenant for the redemption and hope of mankind. The cup of Christ, the new covenant of his blood, has held the place of highest veneration in the Christian faith. In participating in this sacred event, we remember how the Lord's body was broken for us and how the Lord's blood was shed for the remission of sins. Despite our doctrinal and denominational differences, we are united together at the Lord's table. In him, we have redemption through his blood.

Scriptures

Luke 22:15–20

"Then He said to them, "With fervent desire I have desired to eat this Passover with you before I suffer; "for I say to you, I will no longer eat of it until it is fulfilled in the kingdom of God." Then He took the cup, and gave thanks, and said, "Take this and divide it among yourselves; "for I say to you, I will not drink of the fruit of the vine until the kingdom of God comes." And He took bread, gave thanks and broke it, and gave it to them, saying, "This is My body which is given for you; do this in remembrance of Me." Likewise He also took the cup after supper, saying, "This cup is the new covenant in My blood, which is shed for you."

1 Corinthians 11:24–28

"And when He had given thanks, He broke it and said, "Take, eat; this is My body which is broken for you; do this in remembrance of Me." In the same manner He also took the cup after supper, saying, "This cup is the new covenant in My blood. This do, as often as you drink it, in remembrance of Me." For as often as you eat this bread and drink this cup, you proclaim the Lord's death till He comes. Therefore whoever eats this bread or drinks this cup of the Lord in an unworthy manner will be guilty of the body and blood of the Lord. But let a man examine himself, and so let him eat of the bread and drink of the cup."

John 6:51–58

"I am the living bread which came down from heaven. If anyone eats of this bread, he will live forever; and the bread that I shall give is My flesh, which I shall give for the life of the world." The Jews therefore quarreled among themselves, saying, "How can this Man give us His flesh to eat?" Then Jesus said to them, "Most assuredly, I say to you, unless you eat the flesh of the Son of Man and drink His blood, you have no life in you. "Whoever eats My flesh and drinks My blood has eternal life, and I will raise him up at the last day. "For My flesh is food indeed, and My blood is drink indeed. "He who eats My flesh and drinks My blood abides in Me, and I in him. "As the living Father sent Me, and I live because of the Father, so he who feeds on Me will live because of Me. "This is the bread which came down from heaven--not as your fathers ate the manna, and are dead. He who eats this bread will live forever."

Acts 2:42

"And they continued steadfastly in the apostles' doctrine and fellowship, in the breaking of bread, and in prayers."

Acts 20:7

"Now on the first day of the week, when the disciples came together to break bread, Paul, ready to depart the next day, spoke to them and continued his message until midnight."

Matthew 26:26–30

"And as they were eating, Jesus took bread, blessed and broke it, and gave it to the disciples and said, "Take, eat; this is My body." Then He took the cup, and gave thanks, and gave it to them, saying, "Drink from it, all of you. "For this is My blood of the new covenant, which is shed for many for the remission of sins. "But I say to you, I will not drink of this fruit of the vine from now on until that day when I drink it new with you in My Father's kingdom." And when they had sung a hymn, they went out to the Mount of Olives."

Mark 14:22–25

"And as they were eating, Jesus took bread, blessed and broke it, and gave it to them and said, "Take, eat; this is My body." Then He took the cup, and when He had given thanks He gave it to them, and they all drank from it. And He said to them, "This is My blood of the new covenant, which is shed for many. "Assuredly, I say to you, I will no longer drink of the fruit of the vine until that day when I drink it new in the kingdom of God."

John 6:35

"And Jesus said to them, "I am the bread of life. He who comes to Me shall never hunger, and he who believes in Me shall never thirst."

1 Corinthians 10:16–17

"The cup of blessing which we bless, is it not the communion of the blood of Christ? The bread which we break, is it not the communion of the body of Christ? For we being many are one bread, and one body: for we are all partakers of that one bread."

1 Corinthians 10:21–22

"You cannot drink the cup of the Lord and the cup of demons; you cannot partake of the Lord's table and of the table of demons. Or do we provoke the Lord to jealousy? Are we stronger than He?"

Hebrews 4:16

"Let us therefore come boldly to the throne of grace, that we may obtain mercy and find grace to help in time of need."

Quotes

"We who have turned our lives over to Christ need to know how very much he longs to eat with us, to commune with us. He desires a perpetual Eucharistic feast in the inner sanctuary of the heart."
— Richard J. Foster

"Every day He humbles Himself just as He did when from His heavenly throne into the Virgin's womb; every day He comes to us and lets us see Him in lowliness, when He descends from the bosom of the Father into the hands of the priest at the altar."
— St. Francis of Assisi

"If I am to answer the question, 'How would Christ solve modern problems if He were on earth today,' I must answer it plainly; and for those of my faith there is only one answer. Christ is on earth today; alive on a thousand altars; and He does solve people's problems exactly as He did when He was on earth in the more ordinary sense. That is, He solves the problems of the limited number of people who choose of their own free will to listen to Him."
— G.K. Chesterton

"How can you hope to enter into communion with him when at some point in your life you are running away from him?"
— Dietrich Bonhoeffer

"We adore Thee most holy Lord Jesus Christ, here in all Thy Churches, which are in the whole world, because by Thy holy cross, Thou hast redeemed the world."
— St. Francis of Assisi

"The Eucharist is the consummation of the whole spiritual life."
— St. Thomas Aquinas

"Put your sins in the chalice for the precious blood to wash away. One drop is capable of washing away the sins of the world."
— Mother Teresa of Calcutta

"His body and blood have everywhere, but especially at this Sacrament, a true and real presence."

— John Wesley

"Out of the darkness of my life, so much frustrated, I put before you the one great thing to love on earth: the Blessed Sacrament…There you will find romance, glory, honour, fidelity, and the true way of all your loves on earth, and more than that: Death. By the divine paradox, that which ends life, and demands the surrender of all, and yet by the taste—or foretaste—of which alone can what you seek in your earthly relationships (love, faithfulness, joy) be maintained, or take on that complexion of reality, of eternal endurance, which every man's heart desires."

— J.R.R. Tolkien

"I haste to this Sacrament for the same purpose that St. Peter and John hasted to His sepulchre; because I hope to find Him there."

— John Wesley

"Prayer does not consist in an effort to obtain from God the things which are necessary for this life. Prayer is an effort to lay hold of God Himself, the Author of life, and when we have found Him who is the source of life and have entered into communion with Him, then the whole of life is ours and with Him all that will make life perfect."

— Sadhu Sundar Singh

Maxims

- He was broken so we could be whole.
- This is the body of Christ, broken for you.
- This is the blood of the new covenant, shed for the remission of sins.

Discussion Questions

1) Why does the body and the blood have a unifying effect on all

denominations? "We all agree on the sacredness and important of this ordinance, why?"

2) What does it mean that a man or woman should examine themselves before they take from the Lords table?

3) What are the consequences of taking the Lord's Supper in an unworthy manner?

Practical Challenges

1) As a small group, take communion together and pray for each other's needs beforehand.

2) Watch the movie, *The Passion of the Christ*, then take communion together.

Further Study

Bread and Wine, Plough Publishing

The Lord's Supper, William Barclay

Christ and Human Suffering, E. Stanley Jones

God the Rebel, G.K. Chesterton

Life in the Blood, Toyohiko Kagawa and Sadhu Sundar Singh

The Father's Hands, George Macdonald

Poetical Works III, John Wesley

The Life and Teaching of Jesus Christ, James S. Stewart

The Exposition of Holy Scripture, Alexander Maclaren

Written in Blood, Robert E. Coleman

CHAPTER 26: LOVE SLAVES

James, a bondservant of God and of the Lord Jesus Christ.
Jude, the bondservant of Jesus Christ.
Simon Peter, a bondservant and an apostle of Jesus Christ.
Paul and Timothy, the bondservants of Jesus Christ.
Paul, a bondservant of God.

In an age of self-help, independence, and personal rights comes a sobering remembrance of a faith of self-denial. Christ said long ago that *"if any man be my disciple let him take up his cross and follow me."* This model of self-sacrifice for the sake of the Master's house, has been demonstrated by the saints of old. As Paul so aptly stated, *"I bear on my body the marks of Jesus Christ."* These are marks of loyalty, submission, and slavery to the Master's house. A slave has no rights or possessions and no power. However, in this good Master's house, a life surrendered is a life found.

Scriptures

1 Corinthians 9:19–23

> "For though I am free from all men, I have made myself a servant to all, that I might win the more; and to the Jews I became as a Jew, that I might win Jews; to those who are under the law, as under the law, that I might win those who are under the law; to those who are without law, as without law (not being without law toward God, but under law toward Christ), that I might win those who are without law; to the weak I became as weak, that I might win the weak. I have become all things to all men, that I might by all means save some. Now this I do for the gospel's sake, that I may be partaker of it with you."

Matthew 12:30

> "He who is not with Me is against Me, and he who does not gather with Me scatters abroad."

Matthew 20:25–28

"But Jesus called them to Himself and said, "You know that the rulers of the Gentiles lord it over them, and those who are great exercise authority over them. "Yet it shall not be so among you; but whoever desires to become great among you, let him be your servant. "And whoever desires to be first among you, let him be your slave—"just as the Son of Man did not come to be served, but to serve, and to give His life a ransom for many.""

John 15:14–15

"You are My friends if you do whatever I command you. "No longer do I call you servants, for a servant does not know what his master is doing; but I have called you friends, for all things that I heard from My Father I have made known to you."

Romans 8:2

"For the law of the Spirit of life in Christ Jesus has made me free from the law of sin and death."

Romans 6:16–18

"Do you not know that to whom you present yourselves slaves to obey, you are that one's slaves whom you obey, whether of sin leading to death, or of obedience leading to righteousness? But God be thanked that though you were slaves of sin, yet you obeyed from the heart that form of doctrine to which you were delivered. And having been set free from sin, you became slaves of righteousness."

John 13:14–17

"If I then, your Lord and Teacher, have washed your feet, you also ought to wash one another's feet. "For I have given you an example, that you should do as I have done to you. "Most assuredly, I say to you, a servant is not greater than his master; nor is he who is sent greater than he who sent him. "If you know these things, blessed are you if you do them."

Luke 22:27

> "For who is greater, he who sits at the table, or he who serves? Is it not he who sits at the table? Yet I am among you as the One who serves."

Luke 14:33

> "So likewise, whoever of you does not forsake all that he has cannot be My disciple."

Things to Remember Regarding Slavery to Christ

"Worry is the other destructive force stemming from un-yielded rights. Occasions for worry also are *opportunities* for you to discover the faithfulness of the Father. As human beings, we have six basic essentials for living. When we find one of these rights threatened, self-love, (self-preservation), signals danger to the personality. A man who is trying to run his *own* life will worry. He has no heavenly Father's promise of provision, and must take full responsibility for insuring and meeting all these needs himself. He assumes a responsibility that is not rightfully his, and this produces worry."

— From the article, "Free as a Slave," by Winkie Pratney

These six needs are:

> **Acceptance**: A sense of belonging, being well loved, and cared for.
> **Accomplishment**: A longing to do something worthwhile with time, talents, and opportunity.
> **Provision**: Having food, housing, clothes, and money to meet needs and pay bills and taxes.
> **Possessions**: Things we can call our own; belongings to use in the business of living.
> **Safety**: To be protected from hurt, danger or disaster, illness, incapacity, or disability.
> **Security**: Assurance of tomorrow, whatever the future holds; a sense of guidance.

Love Slave

Bondservants/Love slaves in ancient times were slaves who for the love of their master's house impressed themselves into lifetime servitude. This role was the title the apostles chose for themselves and it was this willful sacrifice, which still advances the kingdom today. Winkie Pratney says, "Remember like legal bondage slavery to sin is marked by fear of punishment and hope of reward, as well as guilt and emptiness. Slavery to Jesus has the mark of love - unselfish choices for the highest good of God and his creation."

— Winkie Pratney

Quotes

"The only right a Christian has is the right to give up his rights."

— Oswald Chambers

"Carry the cross patiently, and with perfect submission; and in the end it shall carry you."

— Thomas à Kempis

"God will not come and help men to do their work. He asks that they should give themselves to Him for the doing of His work."

— G. Campbell Morgan

"There is a threefold ministry to which we are called: the ministry of service, the ministry of sacrifice, and the ministry of suffering."

— Samuel Logan Brengle

"Let God have your life; He can do more with it than you can."

— D.L. Moody

"Who cares who frowns, if God smiles."

— Catherine Booth

"From my many years experience I can unhesitatingly say that the cross bears those who bear the cross."

— Sadhu Sundar Singh

"In order to know God, we must often think of Him; and when we come to love Him, we shall then also think of Him often, for our heart will be with our treasure."

— Brother Lawrence

"The greatness of a man's power is the measure of his surrender."

— William Booth

"Their hearts had been bowed and broken by His great love; henceforth they were His bond-slaves no longer free to come and go as they pleased but only as He willed, for the adamantine chains of love held them, and the burning passion of love constrained them. Such bondage and service became the most perfect liberty."

— Samuel Logan Brengle

"The God of holiness and eternal majesty is hardly mentioned these days. The preachers used to declare with holy boldness to the pew dwellers, 'You are lost.' Today it is, 'You are loved.' It takes living men to deliver the living Word. Unless the preachers walk in the fear of the Lord and step out of eternity into the pulpits, the spiritual life of the nation will continue in its descent to weakness and finally apostasy."

— Leonard Ravenhill

"We foolish mortals sometimes live through years not realizing how short life is, and that TODAY is your life."

— Edith Schaeffer

"My yoke is easy, and my burden is light,' said Jesus. And this is His easy yoke and light burden. His yoke is the yoke of love and it is easy. Love makes it easy. His burden is the burden of love and it is light. Love makes it light...To the sinner the yoke looks intolerable, the burden looks unbearable. But to those who have entered into the secret of his Master, His yoke is the badge of freedom, and His burden gives wings to the Soul."

— Samuel Logan Brengle

"If the Lord is glorified the servant is satisfied."

— Winkie Pratney

Maxims

- It's healthy to bow.
- Love finds a need and meets it.
- Serve up and serve down.
- Get comfortable with being uncomfortable.
- If it's difficult, it's probably the cross.
- Meekness is not weakness.
- It's ok to have possessions as long as they don't possess you.

Discussion Questions

1) How is slavery to Christ true freedom?
2) How does suffering and service apply to leadership ?
3) Are the standards for material possessions set by culture or by the Spirit?

Practical Challenges

1) Memorize Winkie's "Six Human Needs" and read his *Free as a Slave* tract (Share them with someone new.)
2) Give something away that your emotionally attached to.
3) Ask the Holy Spirit to reveal to your heart where you are making compromises with your testimony, due to the human need of acceptance.

Further Study

Love Slaves, Samuel Logan Brengle
Free as a Slave, Winkie Pratney

The Seven Spirits, General William Booth
Aggressive Christianity, Catherine Booth
Vanya, Myrna Grant
Humility, Andrew Murray
Something Beautiful for God, Malcolm Muggeridge
True Submission, Charles G. Finney
The Revival Hymn (YouTube)
Celebration of Discipline, Richard Foster
Spiritual Leadership, J. Oswald Sanders
Spiritual Lessons, J. Oswald Sanders
Youth Aflame ("Phillip" Chapter), Winkie Pratney
L'Abri, Edith Schaeffer
Insanity of God, Nik Ripkin

CHAPTER 27: DOCTRINE

In these latter days of heresy and deception, we must earnestly contend for the authentic faith that was once delivered. We must uphold and trust the majestic truths of the Christian faith. We cannot forsake them to the pressures and influences of society and culture, nor can we get sidetracked by dogma and tradition, but must keep our eyes focused on Jesus of Nazareth—the cornerstone of all truth. The church has always acted as the bastion of hope, the steward of truth, and preserver of society. We are the salt of the earth, but if we the church should forsake the doctrines of Christ, we will be trampled under the feet of men.

Scriptures

Acts 20:27

>"For I have not shunned to declare to you the whole counsel of God."

Proverbs 14:16

>"A wise man fears and departs from evil, But a fool rages and is self-confident."

Titus 1:9

>"Holding fast the faithful word as he has been taught, that he may be able, by sound doctrine, both to exhort and convict those who contradict."

Titus 2:1–2

>"But as for you, speak the things which are proper for sound doctrine: that the older men be sober, reverent, temperate, sound in faith, in love, in patience."

Jude 1:3

>"Beloved, while I was very diligent to write to you concerning our common salvation, I found it necessary to write to you exhorting you to contend earnestly for the faith which was once for all delivered to the saints."

1 Timothy 6:3–5
"If anyone teaches otherwise and does not consent to wholesome words, even the words of our Lord Jesus Christ, and to the doctrine which accords with godliness, he is proud, knowing nothing, but is obsessed with disputes and arguments over words, from which come envy, strife, reviling, evil suspicions, useless wranglings of men of corrupt minds and destitute of the truth, who suppose that godliness is a means of gain. From such withdraw yourself."

2 Timothy 1:13
"Hold fast the pattern of sound words which you have heard from me, in faith and love which are in Christ Jesus."

2 Timothy 2:2–3
"And the things that you have heard from me among many witnesses, commit these to faithful men who will be able to teach others also. You therefore must endure hardship as a good soldier of Jesus Christ."

2 Timothy 3:15–17
"And that from childhood you have known the Holy Scriptures, which are able to make you wise for salvation through faith which is in Christ Jesus. All Scripture is given by inspiration of God, and is profitable for doctrine, for reproof, for correction, for instruction in righteousness, that the man of God may be complete, thoroughly equipped for every good work."

2 Timothy 4:2–5
"Preach the word! Be ready in season and out of season. Convince, rebuke, exhort, with all longsuffering and teaching. For the time will come when they will not endure sound doctrine, but according to their own desires, because they have itching ears, they will heap up for themselves teachers; and they will turn their ears away from the truth, and be turned

aside to fables. But you be watchful in all things, endure afflictions, do the work of an evangelist, fulfill your ministry."

1 John 4:1

"Beloved, do not believe every spirit, but test the spirits, whether they are of God; because many false prophets have gone out into the world."

Acts 17:10–11

"Then the brethren immediately sent Paul and Silas away by night to Berea. When they arrived, they went into the synagogue of the Jews. These were more fair-minded than those in Thessalonica, in that they received the word with all readiness, and searched the Scriptures daily to find out whether these things were so."

2 John 1:9–11

"Whoever transgresses and does not abide in the doctrine of Christ does not have God. He who abides in the doctrine of Christ has both the Father and the Son. If anyone comes to you and does not bring this doctrine, do not receive him into your house nor greet him; for he who greets him shares in his evil deeds."

Thoughts on Doctrine

Christocentric theology: All theology must center, focus on, and uplift the character and person of Christ, or it is not true theology.

- Where doctrines divide, Christ unites.
- Always defend the character of God and not your stance or theological position.
- Christ is always to be experienced before espoused (*"But you have not so learned Christ,"* Ephesians 4:20).

Four Foundational Doctrines

These doctrines have stood the test of time:

Salvation
"Man's only hope of redemption is through the shed blood of Jesus Christ the Son of God.

a. Conditions to Salvation. Salvation is received through repentance toward God and faith toward the Lord Jesus Christ. By the washing of regeneration and renewing of the Holy Spirit, being justified by grace through faith, man becomes an heir of God according to the hope of eternal life (Luke 24:47; John 3:3; Romans 10:13–15; Ephesians 2:8; Titus 2:11; 3:5–7).

b. The Evidences of Salvation. The inward evidence of salvation is the direct witness of the Spirit (Romans 8:16). The outward evidence to all men is a life of righteousness and true holiness (Ephesians 4:24; Titus 2:12).

— Constitution of the Assemblies of God, Article V.5"

The Baptism in the Holy Spirit
"All believers are entitled to and should ardently expect and earnestly seek the promise of the Father, the baptism in the Holy Spirit and fire, according to the command of our Lord Jesus Christ. This was the normal experience of all in the early Christian church. With it comes the enduement of power for life and service, the bestowment of the gifts and their uses in the work of the ministry (Luke 24:49; Acts 1:4, 8; 1 Corinthians 12:1–31). This experience is distinct from and subsequent to the experience of the new birth (Acts 8:12–17; 10:44–46; 11:14–16; 15:7–9). With the baptism in the Holy Spirit come such experiences as an overflowing fullness of the Spirit (John 7:37–39; Acts 4:8), a deepened reverence for God (Acts 2:43; Hebrews 12:28), an intensified consecration to God, dedication to His work (Acts 2:42), and a more active love for Christ, for His Word, and for the lost (Mark 16:20).

— Constitution of the Assemblies of God, Article V.7"
Divine Healing

"Divine healing is an integral part of the gospel. Deliverance from sickness is provided for in the Atonement, and is the privilege of all believers (Isaiah 53:4, 5; Matthew 8:16,7; James 5:14–16).

— Constitution of the Assemblies of God, Article V.12"

The Second Coming of Christ
The Blessed Hope
"The resurrection of those who have fallen asleep in Christ and their translation together with those who are alive and remain unto the coming of the Lord, is the imminent and blessed hope of the church," (Thessalonians 4:16-17; Romans 8:23; Titus 2:13; 1 Corinthians 15:51, 52).

— Constitution of the Assemblies of God, Article V.13"

Quotes

"Jesus did not urge his disciples to commit their lives to a doctrine, but to a person who was the doctrine, and only as they continued in his Word could they know the truth."
— Robert E. Coleman

"From time immemorial men have quenched their thirst with water without knowing anything about its chemical constituents. In like manner we do not need to be instructed in all the mysteries of doctrine, but we do need to receive the Living Water which Jesus Christ will give us and which alone can satisfy our souls."
— Sadhu Sundar Singh

"Elegance of language must give way before simplicity in preaching sound doctrine."
— Girolamo Savonarola

"The Gospel is not a mere message of deliverance, but a canon of conduct; it is not a theology to be accepted, but it is ethics to be lived. It is not to be believed only, but it is to be taken into life as a guide."

— Alexander Maclaren

"Truth always carries with it confrontation. Truth demands confrontation; loving confrontation nevertheless. If our reflex action is always accommodation regardless of the centrality of the truth involved, there is something wrong."　　　　— Francis Schaeffer

"Let there be more prayer, more study of the Word, more humility, more acting out what we already know; thus shall we be more united together, not only in love, but in one mind and in one judgment."
　　　　— George Mueller

"Whatever our creed, we stand with admiration before the sublime character of Jesus."
　　　　— E. Stanley Jones

"When a man comes under the blood of Christ, his whole capacity as a man is refashioned. His soul is saved, yes, but so are his mind and his body. True spirituality means the lordship of Christ over the total man."
　　　　— Francis A. Schaeffer

"It is the great business of every Christian to save souls. People complain that they do not know how to take hold of this matter. Why, the reason is plain enough; they have never studied it. They have never taken the proper pains to qualify themselves for the work. If you do not make it a matter of study, how you may successfully act in building up the kingdom of Christ, you are acting a very wicked and absurd part as a Christian."　　　　— Charles G. Finney

"Doctrinal rightness and rightness of ecclesiastical position are important, but only as a starting point to go on into a living relationship— and not as ends in themselves."
　　　　— Francis A. Schaeffer

"You can only learn so much from books. You can only learn so much from education. Ultimately, it is the wisdom of God that will carry you through in the toughest situations of life."

— Ravi Zacharias

"Christianity is not a doctrine, not truth as truth, but the knowledge of a Person; it is knowing the Lord Jesus. You cannot be educated into being a Christian."

— T. Austin-Sparks

"I believe in God the Father Almighty, maker of heaven and earth: and in Jesus Christ his only son our Lord, who was conceived by the Holy Ghost, born of the virgin Mary, suffered under Pontius Pilate, was crucified, dead, and buried: he descended into hell; the third day he rose again from the dead; he ascended into heaven, and sitteth on the right hand of God the Father Almighty; from thence he shall come to judge the quick and the dead. I believe in the Holy Ghost; the holy catholic church; the communion of saints; the forgiveness of sins; the resurrection of the body, and the life everlasting. Amen."

— The Apostles' Creed

Maxims

- Jesus is savior, healer, baptizer in the Holy Spirit, and soon coming king.
- Major on the majors and minor on the minors.
- We fight with ideas and attitudes.
- Chew the meat and spit the bone.
- Intent is prior to content.
- Intellectual deception always follows moral rejection.
- God has spoken, and the rest is just commentary.
- Our faith is not in a what, but in a whom.
- Doctrines should reach, preach, and teach.

Discussion Questions

1) How can doctrine be helpful or harmful to a believer?
2) Is there anything I teach you don't agree with? (You want your disciples to have the freedom and courage to disagree).
3) What does it mean to chew the meat and spit out the bone?

Practical Challenges

1) Memorize the Apostles' Creed.
2) Study the book *Bible Doctrines* by P.C. Nelson.
3) Start being able to support the doctrines you believe with five scripture verses each; let this build to ten each, to twenty each, and so on.

Further Study

Statement of Fundamental Truth, Assemblies of God
Bible Doctrines, P.C. Nelson
What the Bible Teaches, R.A. Torrey
The Fundamental Doctrines of the Christian Faith, R.A. Torrey
Knowing the Doctrines of the Bible, Myer Pearlman
Systematic Theology, Charles G. Finney
Systematic Theology, Ernest S. Williams
The Knowledge of the Holy, A.W. Tozer
The Nature and Character of God, Winkie Pratney
Your Confirmation, J.R.W. Stott
How Shall We Then Live?, Francis Schaeffer (YouTube Series)
The Faith Once Delivered, Ian Macpherson
Dispensational Truth, Clarence Larkin
Sharing your Faith Series (YouTube Series and Booklet), Gordon C. Olson
The Truth Shall Make You Free, Gordon C. Olson
The Philosophy of the Plan of Salvation, J.B. Walker
All the Doctrines of the Bible, Herbert Lockyer
Therefore Stand, Wilbur Moorehead Smith
The God They Never Knew, George Otis, Jr.
Understanding the Atonement for the Mission of the Church, John Driver

CHAPTER 28: THE FOUNDATION

And now abide faith, hope, love, these three; but the greatest of these is love. — The Apostle Paul

When we speak of the foundation of the Christian faith and its cardinal virtues, we must consider the object of these virtues. For it is not faith for the sake of faith, or love for the sake of love, or hope for its own merit; rather, the object of these virtues cannot be anything else but the central figure Jesus of Nazareth. For our faith is ultimately trusting in his person, loving his character, and eagerly hoping for his promised return.

Our faith lived out in a life of loving obedience is not in creed, article, or confession, but rather, is placed solely in the person of Christ. Simply trusting Christ Jesus in every area is the Christian's duty and privilege. Faith is more than just giving intellectual assent to a list of doctrines, but rather, a yielding of allegiance to the character of Christ.

Scriptures

Faith

Habakkuk 2:4

> "Behold the proud, His soul is not upright in him; But the just shall live by his faith."

Romans 10:14–15

> "How then shall they call on Him in whom they have not believed? And how shall they believe in Him of whom they have not heard? And how shall they hear without a preacher? And how shall they preach unless they are sent? As it is written: "How beautiful are the feet of those who preach the gospel of peace, Who bring glad tidings of good things!"

Romans 10:17

>"So then faith comes by hearing, and hearing by the word of God."

Ephesians 2:8–10

>"For by grace you have been saved through faith, and that not of yourselves; it is the gift of God, not of works, lest anyone should boast. For we are His workmanship, created in Christ Jesus for good works, which God prepared beforehand that we should walk in them."

James 2:26

>"For as the body without the spirit is dead, so faith without works is dead also."

Galatians 3:26

>"For you are all sons of God through faith in Christ Jesus."

Romans 5:1

>"Therefore, having been justified by faith, we have peace with God through our Lord Jesus Christ."

John 1:12–13

>"But as many as received Him, to them He gave the right to become children of God, to those who believe in His name: who were born, not of blood, nor of the will of the flesh, nor of the will of man, but of God."

2 Corinthians 5:7

>"For we walk by faith, not by sight."

Hebrews 11:6

>"But without faith it is impossible to please Him, for he who comes to God must believe that He is, and that He is a rewarder of those who diligently seek Him."

Hope

Galatians 5:5

> "For we through the Spirit eagerly wait for the hope of righteousness by faith."

Hebrews 11:1

> "Now faith is the substance of things hoped for, the evidence of things not seen."

Romans 8:24–25

> "For we were saved in this hope, but hope that is seen is not hope; for why does one still hope for what he sees? But if we hope for what we do not see, we eagerly wait for it with perseverance."

1 John 3:3

> "And everyone who has this hope in Him purifies himself, just as He is pure."

Romans 5:1–5

> "Therefore, having been justified by faith, we have peace with God through our Lord Jesus Christ, through whom also we have access by faith into this grace in which we stand, and rejoice in hope of the glory of God. And not only that, but we also glory in tribulations, knowing that tribulation produces perseverance; and perseverance, character; and character, hope. Now hope does not disappoint, because the love of God has been poured out in our hearts by the Holy Spirit who was given to us."

Titus 2: 11–14

> "For the grace of God that brings salvation has appeared to all men, teaching us that, denying ungodliness and worldly lusts, we should live soberly, righteously, and godly in the present age, looking for the blessed hope and glorious appearing of our great God and Savior Jesus Christ, who gave Himself for us, that He might redeem us from every lawless deed and

purify for Himself His own special people, zealous for good works."

1 Peter 1:3

"Blessed be the God and Father of our Lord Jesus Christ, who according to His abundant mercy has begotten us again to a living hope through the resurrection of Jesus Christ from the dead."

Love

1 John 4:16

"And we have known and believed the love that God has for us. God is love, and he who abides in love abides in God, and God in him."

1 John 4:7

"Beloved, let us love one another, for love is of God; and everyone who loves is born of God and knows God."

1 John 2:3

"Now by this we know that we know Him, if we keep His commandments."

John 14:15

"If you love Me, keep My commandments."

John 14:21

"He who has My commandments and keeps them, it is he who loves Me. And he who loves Me will be loved by My Father, and I will love him and manifest Myself to him."

2 John 1:6

"This is love, that we walk according to His commandments. This is the commandment, that as you have heard from the beginning, you should walk in it."

John 3:16

> "For God so loved the world that He gave His only begotten Son, that whoever believes in Him should not perish but have everlasting life."

John 13:34

> "A new commandment I give to you, that you love one another; as I have loved you, that you also love one another."

Quotes

Faith

"Faith, as Paul saw it, was a living, flaming thing leading to surrender and obedience to the commandments of Christ."

— A.W. Tozer

"When a train goes through a tunnel and it gets dark, you don't throw away the ticket and jump off. You sit still and trust the engineer."

— Corrie ten Boom

"Only those who believe obey."

— Dietrich Bonhoeffer

"Fear is faithlessness."

— George Macdonald

"And always our actual position is to be discovered by the way we act, not by the way we talk. We can prove our faith by our committal to it, and in no other way. Any belief that does not command the one who holds it is not a real belief; it is a pseudo belief only. And it might shock some of us profoundly if we were brought suddenly face to face with our beliefs and forced to test them in the fires of practical living."

— A.W. Tozer

"He who loveth God with all his heart feareth not death, nor punishment, nor judgment, nor hell, because perfect love giveth sure access to God. But he who still delighteth in sin, no marvel if he is afraid of death and judgment."

— Thomas à Kempis

"If the Lord fails me at this time, it will be the first time."

— George Mueller

"I know not what He is about to do with me, but I have given myself entirely into His hands."

— Catherine Booth

"Truth that is not undergirded by love makes the truth obnoxious and the possessor of it repulsive."

— Ravi Zacharias

"As I look back over fifty years of ministry, I recall innumerable tests, trials and times of crushing pain. But through it all, the Lord has proven faithful, loving, and totally true to all his promises."

— David Wilkerson

Hope

"Hope and patience are sisters."

— Brother Daniel

"Biblical hope is not wishful thinking or an optimistic outlook; rather, it is a confident expectation based on the certainty of God's Word that as He has anchored us in the past, so He will in the future."

— David Wilkerson

"Do not look to your hope, but to Christ, the source of your hope."

— Charles Spurgeon

"To live without hope is to cease to live."

— Fyodor Dostoevsky

Love

"I have one passion. It is He, only He."

— Count Zinzendorf

"Love is to love the unlovable or it is no virtue at all."

— G.K. Chesterton

"Love is unselfishly choosing for another's highest good."

— C.S. Lewis

"Love finds a need and meets it."

— Brother Daniel

"Faith without love will never save man; but let me say, that true faith is always true love."

— Charles G. Finney

"Love is a command, not just a feeling. Somehow, in the romantic world of music and theatre we have made love to be what it is not. We have so mixed it with beauty and charm and sensuality and contact that we have robbed it of its higher call of cherishing and nurturing."

— Ravi Zacharias

"Where love is, God is."

— Henry Drummond

Maxims

- Faith is simple; trust in God's character.
- Faith is the substance; that substance is Christ.
- Hope and patience are sisters…the reason we have no patience is that we have lost our hope.
- Love by its nature binds itself.
- Love finds a need and meets it.
- Love is to love the unlovable, or it is no virtue all.

- Love is unselfishly choosing for the highest good of another.
- Love is unselfishly choosing for the highest good of God and his kingdom.
- People usually forget what you say, but they will always remember how you treat them.

Discussion Questions

1) Is faith more than intellectual assent, does faith involve the will?
2) How are faith and hope sisters? What is the link between the two?
3) How is faith, hope and love the foundation of the Christian experience?

Practical Challenges

1) Think of the one person in your fellowship that you don't get along with; serve that person as if they were Jesus.
2) Begin to read your Bible out loud; faith still comes by hearing.

Further Study

Four Loves, C.S. Lewis
Orthodoxy, G.K. Chesterton
The Greatest Thing in the World, Henry Drummond
The Changed Life, Henry Drummond
Marathon Faith, John Van Pay
Awake My Heart, J. Sidlow Baxter
God's Smuggler, Brother Andrew
Sadhu Sundar Singh, Cyril Davey
Papers on Godliness, Catherine Booth
Something Beautiful for God, Malcolm Muggeridge
Tramp for the Lord, Corrie Ten Boom
The Heavenly Man, Brother Yun
Smith Wigglesworth: The Apostle of Faith, Stanley Howard Frodsham

CHAPTER 29: FORGIVENESS

"Who is a God like You, Pardoning iniquity and passing over the transgression of the remnant of His heritage? He does not retain His anger forever, because He delights in mercy," (Micah 7:18).

The forgiveness of God expressed in the cross of Christ should create a loving and forgiving people. To harbor unforgiveness and bitterness is to deny the cross of Christ its effectual work in our own hearts and lives. The Messiah said, "he that is forgiven much loves much, and he who loves much forgives much," (Luke 7:47 in paraphrase).

Scriptures

Matthew 18: 21–35
The Parable of the Unmerciful Servant:

> "Then Peter came to Him and said, 'Lord, how often shall my brother sin against me, and I forgive him? Up to seven times?' Jesus said to him, 'I do not say to you, up to seven times, but up to seventy times seven. Therefore the kingdom of heaven is like a certain king who wanted to settle accounts with his servants. And when he had begun to settle accounts, one was brought to him who owed him ten thousand talents. But as he was not able to pay, his master commanded that he be sold, with his wife and children and all that he had, and that payment be made. The servant therefore fell down before him, saying, "Master, have patience with me, and I will pay you all." Then the master of that servant was moved with compassion, released him, and forgave him the debt. But that servant went out and found one of his fellow servants who owed him a hundred denarii; and he laid hands on him and took him by the throat, saying, "Pay me what you owe!" So his fellow servant fell down at his feet and begged him, saying, "Have patience with me, and I will pay you all." And he would not, but went and threw him into prison till he should pay the debt. So when his fellow servants saw what

had been done, they were very grieved, and came and told their master all that had been done. Then his master, after he had called him, said to him, "You wicked servant! I forgave you all that debt because you begged me. Should you not also have had compassion on your fellow servant, just as I had pity on you?" And his master was angry, and delivered him to the torturers until he should pay all that was due to him. So My heavenly Father also will do to you if each of you, from his heart, does not forgive his brother his trespasses."

Proverbs 19:11

"The discretion of a man makes him slow to anger, And his glory is to overlook a transgression."

Matthew 6:12

"And forgive us our debts, as we forgive our debtors."

Colossians 3:13

"Bearing with one another, and forgiving one another, if anyone has a complaint against another; even as Christ forgave you, so you also must do."

Ephesians 4:32

"And be kind to one another, tenderhearted, forgiving one another, even as God in Christ forgave you."

Quotes

"The true Christian is like sandalwood, which imparts its fragrance to the axe which cuts it, without doing any harm in return."
— Sadhu Sundar Singh

"A rattlesnake, if cornered will become so angry it will bite itself. That is exactly what the harboring of hate and resentment against others is - a biting of oneself. We think we are harming others in holding these spites and hates, but the deeper harm is to ourselves."
— E. Stanley Jones

Chapter 29: Forgiveness

"Man has two great spiritual needs. One is for forgiveness. The other is for goodness."

— Billy Graham

"God requires you to love your neighbour as yourself. Again he says, 'let every one look not upon his own things, but upon the things of others.' 'Let every one seek not his own, but another's wealth.' These are express requirements of God; they are the very spirit and substance of the Gospel. Benevolence is a desire to do good to others. A willingness to deny self, for the purpose of promoting the interest of your neighbor, is the very spirit of Christ, it is the heart and soul of his Gospel."

— Charles G. Finney

"The forgiveness of our trespasses can come to us only through His blood…God will give you perfect and full pardon now if you will trust Him, if you will take it of His grace, if instead of attempting to win it, if instead of attempting to merit it you will just come as a poor, guilty, ruined soul—for such you are—and, kneeling at the foot of the Cross, will take God's pardon through Jesus Christ, that is all."

— G. Campbell Morgan

"Nothing can offend those who trust in Christ."

— D.L Moody

"To love means loving the unlovable. To forgive means pardoning the unpardonable. Faith means believing the unbelievable. Hope means hoping when everything seems hopeless."

— G.K. Chesterton

"I firmly believe a great many prayers are not answered because we are not willing to forgive someone."

— D.L. Moody

"No child of God sins to that degree as to make himself incapable of forgiveness."

— John Bunyan

"Bitterness is the seed of Hell."

— Winkie Pratney

"Love endures injury after injury, insult after insult, wrong after wrong, slander after slander, and still keeps right on loving and forgiving and forgetting. It wastes itself in vainly trying to help the unworthy and ungrateful, and still it loves on. That is the first mark of love."

— R.A. Torrey

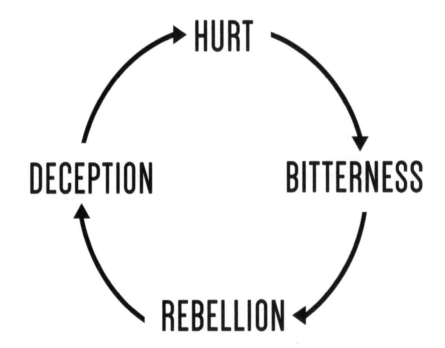

Above: The Bitterness Cycle
Hurt leads to Bitterness; Bitterness leads to Rebellion; Rebellion leads to Deception. The moment you choose to be offended, go directly and privately to who hurt you for reconciliation.

Maxims

- Grief is proportional to intimacy.
- Constant forgiveness.
- Bitterness against someone is like drinking poison expecting the other person to die.
- Hurt people, hurt people.
- He that is forgiven much loves much, and he who loves much forgives much.
- Resolve conflict biblically.

Discussion Questions

1) What is the first thing you should do when you realize you are offended?
2) Can you be right with God, if you're not right with others?
3) What are the signs of bitterness?

Practical Challenges

1) If you have unforgiveness towards someone, start by praying for them. Then follow the next challenge.
2) After you can honestly pray for them, bless them financially.

Further Study

Father Make Us One, Floyd McClung, Jr.
The Hiding Place, Corrie ten Boom
The Suffering of God, Terence Fretheim
Christ and Human Suffering, E. Stanley Jones
Sadhu Sundar Singh, Cyril Davey
The Prodigal, F.W. Boreham
The Cross is Heaven, Sadhu Sundar Singh
The Heavenly Man, Brother Yun
Humility, Andrew Murray
Youth Aflame, Winkie Pratney
A Handbook for Followers of Jesus, Winkie Pratney

CHAPTER 30: THE WAR

"Holy Scripture is full of wars and rumors of wars: The wars of the Lord; the wars of Joshua and Judges; the wars of David, with his and many other magnificent battle songs; till the best known name of the God of Israel in the Old Testament is the Lord of Hosts. And then in the New Testament we have Jesus Christ described as the captain of our salvation. Paul's powerful use of armor and of armed men is familiar to every student of his epistles; and then the whole Bible is crowned with a book all sounding with the battle cries, the shouts and songs of soldiers, till it ends with that city of peace where they hang the trumpets in the hall and study war no more."

— Alexander Whyte

The war involves the reality of the conflict between the kingdom, the Spirit, and the Bride versus the world, the flesh, and the devil.

Scriptures

Philippians 2:10

"That at the name of Jesus every knee should bow, of those in heaven, and of those on earth, and of those under the earth."

Colossians 1:13–14

"He has delivered us from the power of darkness and conveyed us into the kingdom of the Son of His love, in whom we have redemption through His blood, the forgiveness of sins."

Colossians 2:15

"Having disarmed principalities and powers, He made a public spectacle of them, triumphing over them in it."

Revelation 12:11

"And they overcame him by the blood of the Lamb and by the word of their testimony, and they did not love their lives to the death."

Revelation 20:7–10

> "Now when the thousand years have expired, Satan will be released from his prison and will go out to deceive the nations which are in the four corners of the earth, Gog and Magog, to gather them together to battle, whose number is as the sand of the sea. They went up on the breadth of the earth and surrounded the camp of the saints and the beloved city. And fire came down from God out of heaven and devoured them. The devil, who deceived them, was cast into the lake of fire and brimstone where the beast and the false prophet are. And they will be tormented day and night forever and ever."

John 16:33

> "These things I have spoken to you, that in Me you may have peace. In the world you will have tribulation; but be of good cheer, I have overcome the world."

John 14:27

> "Peace I leave with you, My peace I give to you; not as the world gives do I give to you. Let not your heart be troubled, neither let it be afraid."

1 Corinthians 15:57–58

> "But thanks be to God, who gives us the victory through our Lord Jesus Christ. Therefore, my beloved brethren, be steadfast, immovable, always abounding in the work of the Lord, knowing that your labor is not in vain in the Lord."

2 Corinthians 10:4

> "For the weapons of our warfare are not carnal, but mighty through God to the pulling down of strong holds."

Ephesians 6:12

> "For we do not wrestle against flesh and blood, but against principalities, against powers, against the rulers of the darkness of this age, against spiritual hosts of wickedness in the heavenly places."

1 John 2:15–16

> "Do not love the world or the things in the world. If anyone loves the world, the love of the Father is not in him. For all that is in the world--the lust of the flesh, the lust of the eyes, and the pride of life--is not of the Father but is of the world."

Matthew 18:4

> "Therefore whoever humbles himself as this little child is the greatest in the kingdom of heaven."

Revelation 21:1–5

> "Now I saw a new heaven and a new earth, for the first heaven and the first earth had passed away. Also there was no more sea. Then I, John, saw the holy city, New Jerusalem, coming down out of heaven from God, prepared as a bride adorned for her husband. And I heard a loud voice from heaven saying, "Behold, the tabernacle of God is with men, and He will dwell with them, and they shall be His people. God Himself will be with them and be their God. And God will wipe away every tear from their eyes; there shall be no more death, nor sorrow, nor crying. There shall be no more pain, for the former things have passed away." Then He who sat on the throne said, "Behold, I make all things new." And He said to me, "Write, for these words are true and faithful."

Revelation 22:17

> "And the Spirit and the bride say, 'Come!' And let him who hears say, 'Come!' And let him who thirsts come. Whoever desires, let him take the water of life freely."

Convictions that Combat the Darkness

Gratitude

The Spirit of God dwells in a grateful heart, we learn over and over again in the scriptures the wisdom of giving thanks. A grateful person has shifted his interests off himself, unto others and ultimately unto

God. The enemy is not shown one time in the scriptures giving thanks. Rejoice in the Lord always indeed I say rejoice.

Honor

More than just words, a conviction of honor develops a disposition of considering others greater than ourselves. The cardinal ethic of Christianity is sacrifice, this means we must sacrifice the honor we think we are due. We must recognize the great truth that we desperately need each other and that "The last shall be first and the first shall be last." – Jesus the Galilean

Service

In times of great temptation and trial, saints throughout the ages have testified to the wisdom of service. Service towards God and our fellow brothers alleviates our worried hearts, minds and allows us to discover the great kingdom truth "In that by serving others we ourselves are served." – Brother Daniel

Quotes

"From time immemorial men have quenched their thirst with water without knowing anything about its chemical constituents. In like manner we do not need to be instructed in all the mysteries of doctrine, but we do need to receive the Living Water which Jesus Christ will give us and which alone can satisfy our souls."

— Sadhu Sundar Singh

"The whole world knows that His glory has not been spread by force and weapons, but by poor fishermen. It came from God, and so is Christ true, and Christ is thy God, who is in heaven and awaits thee."

— Girolamo Savonarola

"It is that the Spirit is the outbreathing of God, His inmost life going forth in a personal form to quicken. When we receive the Holy

Spirit, we receive the inmost life of God Himself to dwell in a personal way in us. When we really grasp this thought, it is overwhelming in its solemnity. Just stop and think what it means to have the inmost life of that infinite and eternal being whom we call God, dwelling in a personal way in you. How solemn and how awful and yet unspeakably glorious life becomes when we realize this."

— R.A. Torrey

"The inner life is bruised by a running against the laws of the Kingdom. The bruises are guilt complexes, a sense of inferiority, of missing the mark, of being out of harmony with God and with oneself, a sense of wrongness. Divine forgiveness wipes out all that sense of inner hurt and condemnation. Brings a sense of at-homeness-at home with God and oneself, and with life. The universe opens its arms and takes one in. You are accepted—by God, by yourself, and by life. All self-loathing, self-rejection, and all inferiorities drop away. You are a child of God; born from above, you walk the earth, a conqueror, afraid of nothing. Healed at the heart, you can say to life: 'Come on, I'm ready for anything.'"

— E. Stanley Jones

"Let there be more prayer, more study of the Word, more humility, more acting out what we already know; thus shall we be more united together, not only in love, but in one mind and in one judgment."

— George Mueller

"If we think of the Holy Spirit as so many do as merely a power or influence, our constant thought will be, 'How can I get more of the Holy Spirit,' but if we think of Him in the Biblical way as a Divine Person, our thought will rather be, 'How can the Holy Spirit have more of me?'"

— R.A. Torrey

"I do not argue, I only testify: When I belong to Christ and His Kingdom, I am most my own. Bound to the Kingdom, I walk the earth free."

— E. Stanley Jones

"If you're not meeting the Devil head on, then you're going in the same direction"

— Billy Sunday

"It is of the highest importance from the standpoint of experience that we know the Holy Spirit as a person."

— R.A. Torrey

"The Christian warfare is a war between the will and Satan."

— Charles G. Finney

"The Bible mentions three great sources of temptation—the world, the flesh and Satan. The outward world is so correlated to our susceptibilities as to excite them and thus beget a temptation to self-indulgence. The flesh with its appetites and passions clamor for gratification; and hence the flesh and the outward world become temptations. Satan also presents his temptations in every form which subtle malignity can devise."

— Charles G. Finney

"The Devil is a liar."

— Smith Wigglesworth

"Christianity is not a doctrine, not truth as truth, but the knowledge of a Person; it is knowing the Lord Jesus. You cannot be educated into being a Christian."

— T. Austin-Sparks

"The Devil can't get to you, if he can't discourage you."

— Winkie Pratney

Maxims

- Rules without relationship lead to rebellion.
- We fight with ideas and attitudes.

- One person with God is always the majority.
- God's kingdom is founded on inner freedom, not external force.
- God's building an army, not an audience.
- Minister in the opposite spirit.
- The World, Flesh, and Devil is contrary to the Kingdom, Spirit, and Bride

Discussion Questions

1) How important are the promises of God in the battle against darkness ?
2) How do we fight with attitudes and ideas?
3) How does a grateful heart keep us safe?
4) Is there power in the blood of Jesus?

Practical Challenges

1) Pray in the Spirit for twenty minutes every day for a week and see what happens.
2) Dedicate and bless your home.
3) Study and teach the scriptural basis for the final doom of Satan.

Further Study

So Great Salvation, Charles G. Finney
The Holy War, John Bunyan
Satan, F.C. Jennings
The Person and Work of the Holy Spirit, R.A. Torrey
What Meanest This?, Carl Brumback
Power for Life, Jeff Leake
The Spirit of Christ, Andrew Murray
Living in the Spirit, George O. Wood
The Way to Pentecost, Samuel Chadwick
The Root of the Righteous, A.W. Tozer
Parables and Metaphors of Our Lord, G. Campbell Morgan
The Voice the Devil, G. Campbell Morgan
The Pursuit of God, A.W. Tozer
Quiet Talks About the Tempter, S.D. Gordon

Chapter 30: The War

Your Adversary, the Devil, J. Dwight Pentecost
Something Beautiful for God, Malcolm Muggeridge
Destined for the Throne, Paul E. Billheimer
The Bait of Satan, John Bevere
The Strategy of Satan, Warren Wiersbe
Victory over the World, Charles G. Finney
The Unshakable Kingdom and the Unchanging Person, E. Stanley Jones

CHAPTER 31: ABIDING

Considering these things that we have heard in the presence of many witnesses, we must not and shall not allow them to overshadow the Person by whom all of these find their radiance. Christ Jesus the Lord and intimacy with him is the highest ideal, the greatest privilege, for it is the power and life of God. Nothing, absolutely nothing shall take the place of intimacy with him, either religious work, sacrifice, or even the scriptures themselves. We must adopt the wisdom of Solomon's cry, *"Have you seen whom my soul loves?"*

Scriptures

John 15:1–11

> "I am the true vine, and My Father is the vinedresser. Every branch in Me that does not bear fruit He takes away; and every branch that bears fruit He prunes, that it may bear more fruit. You are already clean because of the word which I have spoken to you. Abide in Me, and I in you. As the branch cannot bear fruit of itself, unless it abides in the vine, neither can you, unless you abide in Me. I am the vine, you are the branches. He who abides in Me, and I in him, bears much fruit; for without Me you can do nothing. If anyone does not abide in Me, he is cast out as a branch and is withered; and they gather them and throw them into the fire, and they are burned. If you abide in Me, and My words abide in you, you will ask what you desire, and it shall be done for you. By this My Father is glorified, that you bear much fruit; so you will be My disciples. As the Father loved Me, I also have loved you; abide in My love. If you keep My commandments, you will abide in My love, just as I have kept My Father's commandments and abide in His love. These things I have spoken to you, that My joy may remain in you, and that your joy may be full."

1 Thessalonians 5:17

> "Pray without ceasing."

Galatians 2:20

> "I have been crucified with Christ; it is no longer I who live, but Christ lives in me; and the life which I now live in the flesh I live by faith in the Son of God, who loved me and gave Himself for me."

Colossians 3:3

> "For you died, and your life is hidden with Christ in God."

Colossians 1:27–29

> "To them God willed to make known what are the riches of the glory of this mystery among the Gentiles: which is Christ in you, the hope of glory. Him we preach, warning every man and teaching every man in all wisdom, that we may present every man perfect in Christ Jesus. To this end I also labor, striving according to His working which works in me mightily."

Matthew 11:28–29

> "Come to Me, all you who labor and are heavy laden, and I will give you rest. Take My yoke upon you and learn from Me, for I am gentle and lowly in heart, and you will find rest for your souls."

2 John 1:9

> "Whoever transgresses and does not abide in the doctrine of Christ does not have God. He who abides in the doctrine of Christ has both the Father and the Son."

John 8:31

> "Then Jesus said to those Jews who believed Him, 'If you abide in My word, you are My disciples indeed."

1 John 2:28

> "And now, little children, abide in Him, that when He appears, we may have confidence and not be ashamed before Him at His coming."

1 John 2:6

> "He who says he abides in Him ought himself also to walk just as He walked."

Quotes

"Prayer is continual abandonment to God."

— Sadhu Sundar Singh

"Abide in Jesus, the Sinless One—which means, give up all of self and its life, and dwell in God's will and rest in his strength. This is what brings the power that does not commit sin."

— Andrew Murray

"The dearest friend on earth is a mere shadow compared to Jesus Christ."

— Oswald Chambers

"You need not cry very loud; he is nearer to us than we think…"

— Brother Lawrence

"How can you expect to dwell with God forever, if you so neglect and forsake him here?"

— Jonathan Edwards

"The heart of Paul's religion is union with Christ. This, more than any other conception—more than justification, more than sanctification, more even than reconciliation—is the key which unlocks the secrets of his soul. Within the Holy of Holies which stood revealed when the veil was rent in twain from the top to the bottom on the day of Damascus, Paul beheld Christ summoning and welcoming him in infinite love into vital unity with Himself."

— James S. Stewart

"If God is your own, then all things in Heaven and on earth will be your own, because He is your Father and is everything to you; otherwise you will have to go and ask like a beggar for certain things.

When they are used up, you will have to ask again. So ask not for gifts but for the Giver of Gifts: not for life but for the Giver of Life— then life and the things needed for life will be added unto you."

— Sadhu Sundar Singh

"I drove away from my mind everything capable of spoiling the sense of the presence of God…I just make it my business to persevere in His holy presence…My soul has had a habitual, silent, secret conversation with God."

— Brother Lawrence

"As children, we all had little friends that we thought would last forever, but in a few years the delicate romance passed away and the friends drifted from us. Then came youth with its friendships that we thought were rooted in granite, but they obeyed the same law of change and fleeting. And then came middle life, with its more thoughtful and serious friendship, which after a while were rent with cruel misunderstandings and unexplained silences and so gradually declined. And then we drift on to the lonely, quiet havens of old age, into which we anchor our riper years, to find that change and decay have characterized all earthly things, including what we once supposed were friendships riveted with steel. Like passing ships at sea we lived awhile in the sight of each other's sails, but we each had to make a different port, and so we slipped over the rim of the sea and lost sight of each other. But God is the dear old faithful friend from whom we never sail away and who always is going our way and making for the same port, and whose interests are always our own."

— G. D. Watson

"An infinite God can give all of Himself to each of His children. He does not distribute Himself that each may have a part, but to each one He gives all of Himself as fully as if there were no others."

— A.W. Tozer

"You have to live with Him day by day, and year by year, and to learn to know Him as we learn to know husbands and wives, by continual

experience of a sweet and unfailing love, by many a sacred hour of interchange of affection and reception of gifts and counsels."
— Alexander MacLaren

"The aim of God in history is the creation of an all-inclusive community of loving persons, with himself included in that community as its prime sustainer and most glorious inhabitant."
— Dallas Willard

"You can see God from anywhere if your mind is set to love and obey Him."
— A.W. Tozer

"Each separate member of the passionate few will find his faith so enjoyable, so delectable, so exciting that the very mention of his Savior's name will awaken all his enthusiasm, stir all his devotion, inflame all the faculties of his soul, and shine out lustrously from his very countenance."
— F.W. Boreham

Maxims

- To abide is to reside.
- You're as close to God as you want to be.
- Christ in you is the only hope of your glory.
- Practice his presence.
- To be much like Christ, be much with Christ.
- Set your affections on things above.
- The reason there are so few good speakers of God in the public is that there are so few thinkers about God in private.
- Never let serving God replace knowing God.

Discussion Questions

1) How does this fundamental chapter affect the rest?
2) How is your relationship with Jesus similar to other relationships, how is it different?
3) How does reverence influence your abiding?

Practical Challenges

1) Read *The Practice of the Presence of God* by Brother Lawrence.
2) Set alarms and beep reminders to engage your intimacy with Christ.
3) Spend extravagant time with Jesus daily this will bring his presence into everything. If you cant bring the presence of God into what your doing, stop doing what your doing.

Further Study

The School of Christ, T. Austin Sparks
The True Vine, Andrew Murray
Enjoying Intimacy with God, J. Oswald Sanders
In Christ, E. Stanley Jones
In Christ, A.T. Pierson
The Word Became Flesh, E. Stanley Jones
Abide in Christ, Andrew Murray
The Life of God in the Soul of Man, Henry Scougal
The Christ Life, A.B. Simpson
The Practice of the Presence of God, Brother Lawrence
The Pursuit of God, A.W. Tozer
Christian Living, F.B. Meyer
Christian Book of Mystical Verse, A.W. Tozer
Live Dead Joy, Dick Brogden
The Life of God in the Soul of Man, Henry Scougal
My Utmost for His Highest, Oswald Chambers